MW01252650

THE LOVING HEART

THE LOVING HEART

NAVIGATING THE JOURNEY FROM CONFLICT TO PEACE

Laurie Pappas, PhD

Forward by Gerald Jampolsky, MD

Published by LovingHeart, LLC

P.O. Box 250206
Franklin, MI 48025

www.lovingheartconnection.com

ISBN: 978-0-578-06054-5

Cover Design by Penny Wang
Photography by Debbie Bender Croswell
Graphics by Steve Pappas

This book is printed on ♻ recycled paper.

Printed in the United States of America

Contents

Readers' Comments 7
Acknowledgments 11
Foreword 13
Introduction 15
Chapter 1: Cultivating a Loving Heart 21
Chapter 2: The Spiritual Component 35
Chapter 3: How the Universe Works 51
Chapter 4: The Process of Growth 65
Chapter 5: Inner and Outer Peace 79
Chapter 6: Adversity 91
Chapter 7: Conscious Choice 105
Chapter 8: Tools of the Trade 119
Chapter 9: The Art of True Surrender 151
Chapter 10: Intuition 163
Chapter 11: The Gift of Service 177
Chapter 12: Loving Ourselves 189
Chapter 13: Coping with Strong Emotions 205
Chapter 14: Health and Illness 225
Chapter 15: Relationships 241
Chapter 16: Work and School 259
Chapter 17: Forgiveness 273
Chapter 18: Putting It All Together 287
Bibliography 293
About the Author: Laurie Pappas, PhD 297

Readers' Comments

Reading this book is like opening a treasure chest of timeless teachings that not only will fill your heart with peace and joy but will transform you. After reading this book, I find myself living more lightly. I have learned how to find the gift in adversity, how to trust God even when things seem like they are falling apart, how to forgive myself and others, and most of all, how to choose love in every situation. Laurie's spirit shines through this book as she candidly shares her own struggles and the tools she discovered and utilized to transcend them. Her beautiful message is universal and very much needed in these turbulent times.

Brenda Strausz, MA, LLP
psychologist

When I was in my deepest hour of despair, facing a grave prognosis, my friend and colleague Laurie Pappas took my hand and gave me hope. Her book is a wonderful metaphor to teach us the purpose of life and that when we open our hearts to accept God's grace, miracles abound.

Mark Roby, ND, PAC
doctor of naturopathy

This book comes from the center of Laurie's loving heart. She offers a new approach and hope to those of us who desire to find our way to peace and love. With her light, sweet touch, Laurie's book is a rare treasure infused with her own story. She seems to live what she teaches. This is a beautiful book that shows us that we have the capacity to grow our loving hearts and to live daily with our hearts open.

Joyce Pietila
corporate training consultant

Hope is one of the necessary tools we need when we live in so much stress and turmoil. Dr. Laurie Pappas takes us through her journey from adversity to hope by helping us cultivate a loving heart and make a conscious choice to live peacefully. This book is written with deep thought and clarity to show the process of healing the mind. Dr. Pappas shows us her wisdom and loving spirit in this powerful book for peaceful living.

Susan Thiem
lifestyle coach and facilitator

In this book lies a road map for your journey to finding peace, happiness, and compassionate caring. Dr. Pappas tells it from the heart in a way we can all hear.

Lynn Kasmer, M.Ed
Detroit Public Schools

Reading this book seemed to bring about a peace in me I seldom feel. Though I have been a long-time student of Attitudinal Healing, I still struggle day to day to keep the principles conscious. As Dr. Pappas told her journey, I couldn't help but feel the peaceful connection between our souls, as if she were standing right in front of me. I am grateful to now have a resource to support me in my daily quest for inner peace.

Dave Hodgson
founder and CEO/president, 3-D ETC., Inc.

This book definitely demonstrates how your life is up to you no matter what household you grew up in. The principles described in *The Loving Heart* have helped me with my inner peace and have presented me with ways to use my skills to serve others. I fully believe we are all on this earth to serve each other in some capacity, and this book helps us to do just that.

Lenore Kellner-Smith
IT analyst

After years of spiritual study and reflection, Dr. Laurie Pappas has emerged as an esteemed teacher. The teachings in her book *The Loving Heart: Navigating the Journey from Conflict to Peace* help readers realize their God essence and understand universal principles. Dr. Pappas shows us how to cultivate love in our lives, and she demonstrates that with determination and perseverance, we can heal, learn to love ourselves, and truly change the world.

Ellen Kahn, ND, PhD

In her book *The Loving Heart* Laurie Pappas has succeeded in filling a niche in the personal growth arena by identifying our "loving heart" as the elusive, true nature of the human heart. In plain language, she invites us to recognize our potential to love one another and ourselves. *The Loving Heart* asks us to consider putting love first, above all things that can't love us, such as money, jobs, etc, allowing the love in us to flourish through our very being and seeing what happens. At the very least, we can reap the dividends of a peaceful and harmonious existence.

Tresavon Parker, MA, LLP
clinical psychotherapist

Being powerfully related to others, and noticing and lovingly supplying what is missing, frees and fulfills you. Let the extraordinary Laurie Pappas coach you to give yourself to love. In this amazing book, she gives you both the tools and the courage to be unstoppable.

Barbara Clevenger
Minister, Unity Church of
Farmington Hills, Michigan

Acknowledgments

THE writing of this book has been an exciting and thought-provoking experience, one definitely worth the journey. In all honesty, it has been a team effort, as I reflect on the many people who stood by me throughout. First and foremost, and in deep humility, I pay tribute to the Divine God-Force, without whose words and inspirations this never would have been. My cheering squad has also included many wonderful friends and family members who have urged me on and delighted in this project of mine.

My heartfelt gratitude is given to you, Margaret, Darlene, and Brenda, who have not only supported me in a nonjudgmental and enthusiastic way, but have also given me the confidence and strength needed to complete this undertaking. Susan and Mark, you and the Attitudinal Healing community continue to inspire and sustain me, as you so lovingly encourage my efforts. Debbie, you are genuinely treasured as a friend and a photographer. And to all the people at RJ Communications, my humble appreciation goes to you for guiding me through the complex publishing journey.

Janice, my precious angel of a cousin, you have been a jewel in my life, and Mom (and Dad in spirit), you have made this all possible through your invaluable contributions of personality traits, wisdom, determination, and love.

And lastly, I'd like to thank you, my incredible family whom I adore more and more every day. Steven, you are such an amazingly talented individual, and I truly appreciate the time and effort spent on all the charts in this book. Greg, I am constantly astounded by all that you are able to do, and I am deeply grateful for the love you provide. Zeke, I am so fortified by your choice to curl up loyally on the couch each time I write. Eddie, you are my rock, and it is an honor to share my life with you. From the bottom of my heart, I thank you all!

Foreword

I have known Laurie Pappas for over twenty years. Laurie is the co-founder of the Metro Detroit Center for Attitudinal Healing in Southeastern Michigan. She knows Attitudinal Healing inside out and lives the principles beautifully in her day-to-day life. *The Loving Heart: Navigating the Journey from Conflict to Peace* is written with great passion and empathy, right from the center of her own heart. Her dedication to her spiritual journey and her strong desire to be helpful to others are outstanding.

In my opinion, the wisdom and knowledge contained in this book are helpful to people of all ages, ethnic groups, and cultures, wherever they may be on their spiritual path. In addition, it is a particularly wonderful guide for young adults who are just getting started on their spiritual journey. Laurie writes in an easy to understand language with both richness and depth. What makes this book so special is that the writing comes from the author's personal experiences and is expressed with extraordinary vulnerability and honesty.

When you read this book, you will be inspired to look at the world and yourself differently and to know that it is possible to effect change and to experience inner peace even when there seems to be chaos going on all around you.

—Jerry Jampolsky, MD

Founder, International Center for Attitudinal Healing,
(presently, CorStone Center) Sausalito, California
Author: *Goodbye to Guilt* and *Out of Darkness into the Light*
Co-author with Diane Cirincione: *A Mini Course for Life* and *Finding Our Way Home*

Introduction

IF I could remember my birth, I might recall emerging from the womb with a wide, open heart ready to embrace the world, and at the same time, deeply vulnerable to the emotions and behaviors of everyone around me. My ability to emit love as a child was enormous at times. I could be seen prancing around from person to person, arms outstretched, ready to pour my love out from my core onto whomever was available. At those times, I adored being the bearer of joy and reveled in those moments of benevolence. But then there were the darker periods during which I withdrew into a shadowy shell, as if my survival depended upon some protection mechanism deep at work in the nucleus of the very heart that, a moment ago, had gushed forth its amorous contents. It was as if my heart had two doors—one to loving and the other to fear, and that only one could open at a time.

During my early years, my lack of control over the opening and closing of these doors was apparent and frustrating. I saw myself as overly sensitive and reactive, as did others like my father, who often told me that I had to toughen up. Now, of course, I know that he hurt for me, and that my inner conflict merely triggered his own, over which he, too, often felt helpless.

My family life was filled with expectations, judgments, and demands, a product of the Western culture in which we live and the values and priorities our society holds dear. Competition, high academic standards, and material gain were emphasized, while loving acts were recognized but given little attention. Tempers flared in our house, and arguments over who was right were prevalent. Knowing instinctively that something about this was incorrect, but feeling helpless to change anything, I became depressed and filled with a sense of sadness and foreboding. This I carried with me throughout my teen years and early twenties, becoming bulimic, alcoholic, and addicted to tranquilizers in order to dull my aching heart. It seemed that my pain was just too unbearable to look at, and I wanted to drown it out at any cost.

In my late twenties, more than thirty years ago, I finally surrendered in frustration to a God I didn't know, but who I hoped would be there for me. Little did I realize then how powerful that act of surrender was. It would lead me into a world of knowledge and personal awareness that would not only ease my pain, but would also guide me to work with others who could learn from and respond to this knowledge in the same way that I had. So began a life-long journey of wonder and amazement, demonstrating to me time and again that I had the power and ability to open the door to love in my heart and keep it open much of the time, while gradually clearing out the contents behind the door to darkness.

As my journey began, I first investigated psychotherapy, working with several different kinds of counselors. This seemed to improve my ability to function and helped me begin to see myself in a new light. With help, I was able to explore some of the anger and fear that had kept me stuck for so long, in order to move on with my life. But traditional psychotherapy was only part of the answer for me. I longed to know more. I wanted to understand who I really was, where I came from, and what my purpose here was. I wanted to understand the world we live in, and to learn how best to contribute something to the welfare of mankind. Families like mine, I knew, weren't unusual. Actually, as I looked around, I saw what we all see: war, famine, hurricanes, poverty, illness, lack of harmony in human relationships, and a whole other host of earthly challenges. Plain and simple, I saw that human beings were suffering, and I was determined to find ways to help alleviate this universal pain and anguish, starting with the remaining distress inside of me.

My longing led me further along a spiritual path that would facilitate my ability to find inner peace and extend it outward. I was led to study metaphysics, Attitudinal Healing, A Course in Miracles, Buddhism, and Unity philosophy. My connection to God (or a higher power) became all important to me, and I found myself drawn to assist others in discovering that same connection within them that they could call upon for strength, wisdom, serenity, protection, and stability.

This book, then, is essentially a collection of accumulated learnings over thirty years of living experience. It is not meant to provide "the" answer, because for every person there is a unique set of remedies that are just right for that person. I've come to understand that there are no "right" answers, just ones that work for each of us. I do not claim to have all the answers because I realize that knowledge unfolds as we travel along our evolutionary path, and sometimes I realize that the more I know, the more there is to know. What I would like to do here is merely share my experience with you in the hopes that you might find some of what you're looking for in these pages.

The ideas presented here are ancient truths that have been used for centuries by persons searching for peace within, and they have been applied to the healing of relationships between individuals and between groups of individuals. I have often felt wonder and amazement in my work with clients and students when this knowledge has been applied to their daily lives. I have witnessed dramatic personal transformations, and I am grateful every day for having been given such knowledge.

My sense is that we are each blessed to be living at such a powerful time in history, and that we each have the opportunity to make a significant contribution to the healing of this planet. As we begin our journey in the new millennium, the interval of time that spans the two thousands, it is useful to note that the number 2 in numerology represents partnership—a coming together or joining in order to accomplish a certain task. Cooperation, harmony, and communication are key here, as these are the tools of a working brotherhood of souls intent upon creating change in a world that so desperately needs it. The 2 requires that we move forth from the "me" world to the "us" world, that we care just as much about the welfare of others, as ourselves, and that we treat ourselves well, so that we can be of greater benefit to all those whom we encounter. This millennium is a time of honest, harmonious communication that unifies instead of separates. We are coming together as a human race to face serious world challenges, and all inner grievances and conflicts that refuse to support this communication must be released and ultimately healed. In order to do this, we must start by creating peacefulness inside so that this inner peace can be extended outward.

These pages can facilitate this process. The chapters are designed to be informational as well as experiential, for we gain knowledge not just through reading words and intellectualizing, but through the application, contemplation, and utilization of the written material. Until the principles outlined here are experienced, they are only beliefs, and beliefs are debatable. However, when someone has personally tested an idea and witnessed its truth, there is a "knowingness" that follows. Knowingness provides strength of conviction and impact to a concept, and it necessitates no further debate within.

Thus, these chapters include experiential exercises intended to help you make use of the material in a more holistic way, with the goal of creating knowingness within. While our lives are busy, we often balk at going the extra mile because of time constraints. I urge you to work in whatever way you are able to practice these truths through doing the exercises. Whether you put five or forty-five minutes a day into this, or whether you create a once- or twice-weekly practice session, the quantity of time is not important. What really makes a difference is your commitment to the process. I have learned that not only is peace possible, but with the right tools, anyone can find it with patience, determination, and persistence.

It is helpful to remember that opening one's heart to love is a sacred journey, one to be honored and nurtured with kindness. We may meet with resistance along the way or be ready to give up. We may experience frustration, lack of patience, or disappointment. These circumstances are completely natural, but if we endure and treat ourselves gently, they will pass quickly, and we will regain our composure and our confidence in the process. Keeping this in mind, let's begin a most remarkable voyage into the deeper realms of being.

Each of us can make a difference
When we teach only love
When we commit ourselves to have a heart
That beats only with compassion
Where caring for one another becomes
Our only passion
— Gerald Jampolsky

CHAPTER 1

Cultivating a Loving Heart

GIVEN the state of the world in which we live, when I mention opening our hearts to love, many people either laugh, resist, or plug their ears. Others will give my statement some credence, although loving will often fall at the bottom of their list of priorities, following subjects like defense, who's to blame, ending war, building the economy, or eliminating poverty. No doubt, all of these subjects require contemplation, discussion, and action. However, trouble always has a root cause, and underlying sources such as anger, rage, fear, jealousy, indifference, helplessness, shame, and the like stand in the way of efficient resolution. The antidote to all of these is essentially the development of a kind and loving heart toward all, including ourselves.

The world is changing before our eyes. Human beings have the capacity to think consciously about what we've created, what has worked, and what has not. For centuries, we have been feuding with one another, through war after war—between countries, co-workers, family members, friends, businesses, institutions, and schoolmates.

For the first time in history, enough human beings have reached a stage of consciousness sufficiently evolved to enact significant change in the way we conduct the affairs of life.

Imagine, for a moment, a world filled with loving, understanding, the ability to step into another's shoes, and the desire and motivation to do so. Envision people caring for each other as much as they care for themselves, willing to look at fear directly and compassionately. Picture humanity being as much concerned with *giving* as with *getting*. Under such circumstances, government and all other organizations would work more efficiently, as commissions of people would assemble with the purpose of helping each other to help the world. Each team member might be thinking, "What would my colleague need in order to be the most effective aide for the difficulties we're facing, and what would I need as well?" What if they listened to each other with open hearts and with the aspiration to truly understand the other's point of view—his aching, her pain, his fury, her frustration? What if those who needed help were listened to with empathy and compassion and could really *feel* and *know* that others wanted to be of assistance to them?

Love is the most powerful force in nature. It is also the most healing. When, in the animal kingdom, a baby is not given the nurturing it needs at birth, it fails to thrive. To be able to give and receive love is the most essential component of survival for all living beings. In order to prosper economically, politically, and socially, our planet plainly needs love. Why is this? Because at some sacred region of the innermost depth of our being resides the ability to heal, to blossom, and to flourish, and contact with this dynamic and powerful vital force is found only through opening the channels to a loving heart. When we are in a state of love, we are at our best. Not only do we feel peaceful, but we are able to access the most profound stores of creativity, intuition, and reason, all major ingredients for success on every level.

If you are reading this book, it has arrived in your hands by no accident and out of your desire for inner peace and a commitment on some level to contribute to a movement that is bringing a new way of thinking to our world, one focused on healing from the inside out, one certain to change the way we humans do business, and one that has the potential to pull the world together in a joint effort to make a vast and extraordinary difference such as we have never known. Mankind is made up of individuals, and the happiness and inner peace of those individuals is the driving force behind all that happens here. Opening our hearts to love creates joy, contentment, and tranquility. Peace is its product and harmony its result.

Opening our hearts to the love that resides there, just like gardening, sculpting, or painting, is an art that requires education, practice, and time for development. Remember when we were little children and were learning to ride a bike? It took time, coordination, help, and support, and much falling off and getting back on. Learning to love completely and unconditionally is similar, as it is a process longer and more complex than riding a bike. It may take a lifetime, but we improve as we go along. This means we become happier, more peaceful, and more masterful through time. Life becomes easier and more pleasurable for us and for all those we touch.

With this in mind, then, let's begin our journey with some key concepts that will prepare us for our voyage to inner peace, harmony, and compassionate caring. The first of these involves the universal nature of love.

LOVE IS OUR CORE ESSENCE

Many of us have grown up with the notion that people are inadequate, imperfect, or incompetent. Some of us believe that people are either good or bad, benevolent or evil, decent or corrupt. Certainly, when we look around us, this may appear to be true, depending on the behavior we witness. Religious education may focus on our "sins," and the media may provoke our anger over stories of burglary, murder, or deceit.

However, *A Course in Miracles,* Attitudinal Healing, Buddhism, and other ancient spiritual philosophies paint a very different picture, guiding us to see that what lies at the core of each and every living being is love. That is, if we look beneath any poor behavior, and if we look hard enough, we will find that love exists in every heart everywhere, even though its ability to manifest is different for everyone. This is because some of us are more in tune with this part of us than others.

For many, this sacred loving energy is well hidden under layers and layers of fear, wounding, and pain. When a child of any animal species lacks proper care, it fails to thrive, as we have said. In this case, given its choices and the agony it may have undergone, the child may unconsciously choose to close off his heart so that he can shut off his feelings. In other words, it may be too painful to bear these emotions, and the child may feel unsafe doing so.

A client of mine was abused so badly during childhood that she numbed her emotions, spending many years in anguish over feeling unable to love and constantly fighting urges to behave violently. For certain, she was one of the lucky ones, as she worked hard to overcome her childhood trauma and after several years of therapy was quite successful. Of course, there are others who are unable, unwilling, or incapable of rising above their early experiences and lash out at society or at their co-workers or family members. Some become depressed and withdrawn, retreating from life in a myriad of ways. When I was young, I often became despondent and saw no safe outlet for my emotions. Sometimes I was so wrapped up in myself in the attempt to survive, that my lovingness was nowhere to be seen.

Whatever the behavior, however, love resides in our hearts and is the foundational energy for every cell in our body. Why is this? It is because each of us is a part of a "Universal Spirit energy" that is composed of pure love. Attitudinal Healing's first principle states, *The essence of our being is love.* This demonstrates the notion that all living beings are made of the same material, even though that substance may be invisible to our human eyes. If you put your palms together without touching them to each other, and move them back and forth, away from each other and toward each other, you will feel this energy in the form of heat, pressure, or sensation. This energy, although unseen, forms the basis of who we are, and connects us all to one another because there are no firm boundaries between energies. To the contrary, energies merge with one another, bonding us to the whole kingdom of life form.

There is a story I've been told that helps me visualize this shared essence of who we are. In 1957 in Bangkok, a group of monks from a monastery had to relocate their massive, ten and a half foot tall, 2.5 ton Buddha from their temple to a new location to make way for a new highway being built through the city. They used a crane to lift the idol, but it began to crack, and then rain began to fall. The head monk was concerned about damage to the sacred Buddha, and he decided to lower the statue down to the ground and cover it with a large canvas tarp to protect it from the rain.

Later that evening, the monk went to check on the Buddha. He shined a flashlight under the tarp, and noticed a gleam reflected through a crack in the clay. Wondering about what he saw, he got a chisel and hammer, and began to chip away at the clay. The gleam turned out to be gold, and many hours later the monk found himself face to face with an extraordinary, huge solid gold Buddha.

Historians believe that several hundred years before this, the Burmese army was about to invade Thailand, then called Siam. The monks covered their precious statue with an eight-inch layer of clay to disguise its value. Very likely the Burmese slaughtered all the Siamese monks, and the secret of the statue's golden essence remained intact until that day in 1957.

We are all like the golden Buddha, in some way. We are covered with a protective layer, often so well covered that we have forgotten how to remember our true value.

TAKING RESPONSIBILITY

I remember many times earlier in my life when I felt angry and frustrated over the ways that others behaved, and I recall thinking that if only they would change, I would be happy. If only my parents would stop fighting, if only my friends would call me more, if only my dad weren't so critical, if only my husband would pay more attention to me, if only my kids would clean up their rooms without being reminded, I would be fine. I spent a great number of years focusing on my fury, hurt, or resentment at being treated poorly. During that time, I felt nothing but misery. But somewhere along my path, I realized that the energy I put into *others* changing could better be utilized by altering my expectations in each situation and working on *my own reactions* to others' behavior. In this way, I would no longer set myself up for disappointment, and I would let go of the attempt to manipulate that over which I had little or no control. It was more useful to work on myself than on others, because with myself, *I* was in complete command, no one else.

For most of us, living in this world has taught us to seek gratification of our needs through some outside source. Needs such as love, reassurance, respect, support, understanding, appreciation, and acceptance are important for our emotional and physical well-being, and we tend to go through life looking for these everywhere but inside of us. Even if we're fortunate enough to find someone who gives us most of this, there is always the possibility and even the probability that this person will fail to meet our expectations. This is because human beings have been educated erroneously and will not always act in loving ways even though they may be doing the best they can at any given moment.

Therefore, our real task is to take responsibility for our own happiness by agreeing to do whatever it takes to mend our hearts, including being willing to observe, explore, and release the fear and antagonism that block our happiness. Our *true power* lies inside of us! The key to contentment lies not *out there* somewhere, but right here in our own backyard. We are beautiful creatures, and within each of us is the capacity to reach out to ourselves and to others with kindness. It is this ability to open our hearts that brings us the peace we so desire. With the opening of our hearts, we usher in the warm glow of satisfaction, the bright fire of delight, and the calm ecstasy of having experienced our connection with another human being.

HEALING INTO LOVE

According to the dictionary, *healing* in the nonphysical sense of the word, means to "repair and restore to wholeness" or to "rectify something that causes discord and animosity." When we refer to the term *healing into ove,* we are recognizing that love is a state of mind that is whole, in which no discord or animosity exists, and that there is a healing process through which this can and does occur. This is the healing we will be referring to throughout this book.

If love is the natural and whole state of our being, then what is its opposite? Attitudinal Healing refers to the state of fear as being love's reverse, and sees fear residing underneath all negative emotions. Buddhism uses the term *suffering* to describe this state, and *A Course in Miracles* speaks of an ego state of mind as being the opposite of the God state of mind.

For purposes here, I refer to these two very different emotional or mental states as fear-based consciousness, or love-based consciousness. This is because human consciousness consists of thought energy that has been passed down from generation to generation. This thought energy is composed of beliefs that have been agreed upon by groups of individuals. For example, long ago many people in the old world believed that the earth was flat. Later, with discoveries by explorers such as Columbus and Marco Polo, that belief changed through solid evidence to the contrary. The evidence we use here to change our beliefs or thought systems requires inner proof; that is, through individual experimentation and observation with our own thought systems and their consequential emotional states, we discover what brings us peace of mind and what does not. Keep in mind that thought energy is a creative force, and deeply influences our emotional well-being. In other words, thoughts or attitudes produce feelings.

Through education and experimentation, I have been able to form new beliefs based upon what causes me to feel calm and content or agitated and troubled. These beliefs have been tried and tested many times over by me and people with whom I work, so that a knowingness has formed within. This knowingness generates love-based thoughts and behavior or love-based consciousness.

What does this process of education and experimentation look like? As human beings, we all think erroneously about the nature of reality. We often see ourselves as separate from each other and separate from God. We have forgotten that we are part of God's Divine loving energy, which, unlike our bodies, is invisible and all-powerful. To see ourselves as separate from this energy is to feel disconnected and isolated, which causes a state of fear or conflict.

The process of remembering who we are is one of acknowledging and releasing negative emotions that block our ability to see ourselves and others as we truly are. During this process we study new ways to view reality, experiment with new behaviors and insights, and allow ourselves to feel and release harmful feelings. Every so often along this path, our perceptions will shift and we will see clearly in that moment. This is what we term a *healing*. To heal into love, then, is to see only through the eyes of love, or to be in a state of love-based consciousness.

When we are in love-based consciousness, our thought and speech vocabulary is modified to eliminate certain words and introduce others. For instance, when we are functioning from the mode of fear-based consciousness, we may use words such as *mistake, bad, sin, failure, should, shouldn't, ought, oughtn't, messed up,* etc. These are judgmental words that are not purely loving in their nature. When we are in a state of loving consciousness, we realize that these concepts do not exist. We are not bad, nor have we sinned, failed, or messed up anything. We are simply doing the best we can with what we know at any given moment, and we are being given the exact circumstances we need to heal our hearts at all times. There is nothing we should or shouldn't *do*, *eat*, or *give* and nowhere we should *go* or *be* based upon anyone else's advice and/or command. Love-based consciousness would have us look inside of ourselves for the wisdom that already resides there in order to receive direction, for it is only within the depths of our being that we can hear or feel the guidance that leads us to a more peaceful state of mind.

Healing into love therefore develops over time with practice, patience, perseverance, and support. Shifting from one state of consciousness to another is not something that happens over night, but it can be the task of a lifetime. Learning to revel in those victorious moments when our hearts open and the love comes pouring out, is a crucial part of the journey. To berate ourselves when we close our hearts serves no purpose other than to cause us misery. Only love is the healer and has the power to transform conflict into peace.

LEARNING THROUGH EXPERIENCE

A. Ask yourself the following questions or discuss with a partner:

1. *How open is my heart to love?*
2. *How open is my heart to pain?*
3. *What specifically causes me to close my heart?*
4. *What help do I need to open to love?*
5. *Where or with whom do I feel safe?*
6. *Under what circumstances am I loving to myself?*
7. *Under what circumstances am I unloving to myself?*

B. Guided Meditation

For all guided meditations, you may wish to tape the words and play them back to yourself. Or, you may read a paragraph, close your eyes, and follow its instructions before going on to the next paragraph.

Guided Meditation on Love

Sit comfortably in a quiet place, close your eyes, and allow yourself to breathe deeply and freely. Focus on your breath for a few minutes, letting go of any tension you might feel, until you feel relaxed. If it is difficult to relax, you might try putting on soft music, lighting a candle, and looking at the flame, or doing this in a hot bath. However you can help yourself to relax, do so now.

Now begin by imagining that everyone you know is here, standing in front of you. This includes family and friends that you deeply love, people that you respect or admire, others that you don't know very well but like, and individuals that you find annoying or difficult. Now add to these, extending as far back as you can see, all other beings that you don't know, but that share this Earth with you.

Understand that all of these people want to be happy and peaceful just like you. They are each here doing the best they can with what they know, even the angry or cruel ones. How wonderful it would be for yourself and others if you could love them all. Remember that these individuals are each attempting to do as well as they can with their lives, and that their consciousness is a product of teachings that have been passed down from generation to generation.

Now from your heart center, generate a feeling of love. You may sense this energy emanating from the core of your being, you may visualize glowing light or color, or you may feel warmth radiating outward. It may be helpful to think of someone of whom you are very fond or an animal for whom you feel great tenderness.

Remember to include yourself in the circle of your love. Loving yourself means accepting yourself as you are, with all of your weaknesses and limitations, forgiving whatever you perceive to be your past mistakes, and knowing you did the best you could with what you knew at the time. In addition, realize that it is easier to love others when you are kind to yourself. So see yourself as joyful and happy, with all good being bestowed upon you. See yourself embraced by the warmth and luminosity stemming from your heart center.

Now allow your love to flow out to all the people you have visualized. Begin with the people you care for deeply, and let your bright, loving energy enfold them, body and mind. See them immersed in the glowing warmth of your tenderness, profoundly moved by the touch of your loving.

Next, include those persons you admire or respect and even the ones you hardly know at all.

Now, if you can, extend this compassion to those people that, for you, are the most difficult to care about. Perhaps they are violent or deceitful, manipulative or demanding. Recognize that even these human beings deserve to be loved, and that love may free them from the fear and confusion that cause them to behave the way that they do. Wish for them happiness and inner peace and to be free of their suffering. Don't worry if this is difficult for you. It may take much practice and many years of work to find love in our hearts for those who have hurt us or others. The purpose here is just to entertain the idea of caring about these people and setting an intent.

Now, to the best of your ability, see your love encircling all the beings in your imagination—all those who are tired, ill, hungry, poverty-stricken, lonely, oppressed, afraid, or dying. Understand that all of these circumstances are due to erroneous thinking, and that each of these beings are feeling separate and isolated and greatly in need of being loved and cared for. Send out your prayers and wishes for their healing, for them to return to their wholeness. See the soothing light of your love allay their fears and quiet their hearts.

In conclusion, know that there exists in your heart a boundless ocean of love and that all you must do to reach it is to release what is keeping it from manifesting. Commit yourself to releasing any fear, anger, judgment, annoyance, or sadness that blocks your natural love essence from being revealed. Know that this is the road to peace and it is possible for anyone to get there. Now bring this loving energy back into the present moment and stay with it as long as possible. Thank yourself for allowing these sacred moments to tune into a most powerful inner realm and know that you can return here any time you wish.

It is impossible for you to be
separated from your spiritual nature.
No matter how alone you may feel,
you are never truly alone,
for you live, move, and have your
being in spiritual consciousness.
—Douglas Bloch

CHAPTER 2

The Spiritual Component

I grew up the middle of three girls in a high achieving and demanding Jewish family. We lived in a suburb of Cleveland, Ohio, where living was comfortable and people were used to the finer material pleasures of life. Other than going to religious school each week and attending High Holy Day services once a year, our household was noticeably lacking in its attentiveness to spirituality. In its place, the gods of my upbringing seemed to be productivity, accomplishment, good looks, dressing appropriately, and making sure one conformed to acceptable standards.

Through my years of study, I have discovered this to be a common experience for many due to the often-misguided goals of the culture in which we live. I have also come across many others who have had the opposite experience of growing up with much religious dogma, which held little or no meaning for them. Whether we grew up with too much religion, too little, or just enough, I have found that it is one's concept of spirituality and its practice that plays an all-important role in the development of happiness and peace of mind. I have also discovered that religion can enhance or detract from living life with fullness and grace. Therefore, it is valuable to examine the true meaning of spirituality, and look at how it relates to aspects of religious traditions that are common in our society.

WHAT IS SPIRITUALITY?

We are each part of something much larger and more magnificent than our small bodies and minds. We are, at all times, connected to a Divine energy that is a great deal more powerful and loving than we could ever imagine. As I've come to know it, spirituality is the attempt to know this God-force or Spirit within ourselves, and to understand our greatness as creatures of Divine nature. This occurs as a *sensing* or an *intuition* of a higher presence and direction coming from within. It is a knowingness that something we can neither see nor hear, taste nor touch, is deeply at work within our psyche. And, although we may not be able to identify this with our usual senses, we each have a sixth sense of sorts that can recognize this miraculous trait that we all possess.

When I was about nine years old, I was quite unhappy and disillusioned with the concept of God. I figured God didn't exist because I would pray and still be sad. I also came from a very scientific family who based truths only on knowledge that could be measured or seen. I had heard that there was such a thing as God, but it had no meaning for me because I hadn't experienced its truth on the *inside.* It wasn't until I was in my late twenties and trying desperately to conceive a child that I found my truth. My husband and I had been actively seeking to become pregnant, with no success, for six years. We were about to give up and had applied to adopt a child when I was given Raymond Moody's books, *Life after Life* and *Life after Death.* These were books about

Dr. Moody's research with patients who had suffered near-death experiences. When I read these heartfelt stories about people seeing a bright light and feeling comforted by an amazing peaceful presence, I began to question my former beliefs about God.

Two weeks before I became pregnant with my first child, I remember sitting by a lake in the neighborhood in which I grew up, and having a conversation with a God whose existence I doubted, but who I hoped would show up for me. I told this imaginary friend that I didn't know how to believe in a Spirit or anything beyond myself, but that if I could be given a sign that was undeniable, then I would never question God's presence again. Two weeks later, of course, it was confirmed that I was indeed pregnant, and I had my proof. For me, it was a simple affirmation that I was on the right track again and that I needed to attend to my spiritual needs.

It doesn't happen in such a dramatic way for everyone, but when we discover the truth that we are much more than we think, and that there is actually a force within us that works for our highest good at all times, we are on our way to a faith-filled life. Such a life is filled with the realization that we are highly protected at all times and that some sort of Divine force resides within to carry us through any life challenges that occur. This Divine force has been given many different names by various cultures and ethnic groups who have discovered its presence. Whatever we choose to call it, be it God, Buddha, Christ, Jesus, Moses, Allah, Mohammed, Jehovah, Higher Power, Great Spirit, Higher Mind, Higher Intelligence, Divine Source, Higher Consciousness, Inner Guidance, or Love, it is the same source of energy that has powered all living beings for eternity.

I have found that in order to have a relationship with this part of us, it helps to give it a name. That way we can converse with it, feel it as a part of us, and distinguish it from our everyday personality, which is often unaligned in thought and belief with this higher, wiser, and more loving part of us. Whatever term is comfortable for us seems the best to use. We might pick from among the above listed names, or designate a term that is our own created version. Whatever you decide, make sure that the title you've given this Divine energy is one which feels tender, powerful, and peace filled—not one that carries with it thoughts of guilt, anger, judgment, and the like. If you've grown up with the latter kind of God in your life, find a new term that fits for you now—one that carries new associations and new life.

Once we have a name for this entity within us, we can begin to develop our faith by spending a little time each day communing with this part of us through prayer, contemplation, meditation, etc. This will be covered in more detail later in chapter 9. But for our purposes here, we might want to remember the following: the God-force is a purely loving energy that always seeks our happiness and peace of mind. By tapping into this power, we are attracting to us the very experiences and assistance we need to bring about comfort and a feeling of well-being. This Divine intelligence is perfected in its sense of what we need and is our permanent and unswerving ally at all times. To make use of this natural internal force is a magnificent blessing to us and to all those we touch in our everyday lives.

RELIGION

Religion and religious institutions can be a very important part of our lives. They provide community, moral direction, and something to believe in. These are valuable to us as human beings because we are always searching to improve our lives and live more contentedly. Community gives us a sense of belonging, moral direction supplies a much needed map for human behavior, and something to believe in provides an anchor to hang onto in times of trouble or crisis.

Growing up in the Jewish tradition, for me, had its advantages. Jewish community provided a definite sense of belonging for me, and ritualistic ceremonies such as bar and bat mitzvahs, weddings, funerals, and Jewish holidays were unifying experiences, filled with joy and sadness, but always an avenue for connection with each other. The Jewish concept of giving back to our communities, or of "repairing the world" in some way lent guidance and emboldened me to step out into a troubled world with the intent of helping the poor and undernourished, as well as those who were burdened or oppressed by life's harshness. Finally, the idea of one God who is recognized as the creator and governor of the Universe offered the possibility of consolation during times of distress and guidance for all of life's activities. Christianity, Buddhism, Islam, Hinduism, Taoism, and other religions of the world can provide much the same comfort and guidance for their followers, as many of my students, friends, and clients have confirmed.

However, religion can be interpreted in an enormous variety of ways, and some paths of interpretation are less beneficial than others. For instance, some recognize only their own tradition as the correct one. Under such circumstances, religious wars, conflict, ethnic cleansing, harsh judgment, or fanaticism can occur. In these cases, religion is being used as a weapon against others instead of as a healing agent used to unite.

In less extreme cases, religious dogma may cause guilt, shame, anger, or fear among participants. Some of us have been raised in environments in which religious rules have governed our lives. Perhaps we learned these in religious schools or from ministers, rabbis, priests, or parents. But if we have been expected to follow these imperatives without question or discussion, we may arrive at a place of confusion followed by a whole host of negative emotions that seem to run our lives.

In other cases, the use of language itself can have harmful effects. Each year when I would go to High Holy Day services according to the Jewish tradition, I would read aloud from a holy book all the ways in which I had "sinned" as a human being. And I would offer my sincere apologies. Although much of this was intended to improve people's behavior, it caused many much shame and embarrassment, leading to self-effacement, inner criticism, and lowered tolerance for others. I have since learned that the mere act of rephrasing, eliminating, or substituting vocabulary could make an immensely positive difference in the way we relate to ourselves and to others. By seeing ourselves as always doing the best we can, but continually striving to improve ourselves, we can undo the damage that a word like *sin* might cause.

For religion to work well, we must each be allowed to come to our own conclusions and act on them as well, instead of feeling pressure to do as we're told. We must be able to ask questions when we're confused and seek answers until we're satisfied that the answers bring us comfort and peace. And finally, we must receive instruction on how to commune with the Divine presence within us in order to discover truths about what works for us and what does not. There are those who follow a particular religious philosophy and allow others to do as they choose, but deep within they are judgmental of the choices that others make. In my experience, that is not a beneficial use of religious practice. To observe a specific faith and adhere to the principles of love and nonjudgment for all is the healthiest and most constructive use of religion.

SPIRITUAL GROWTH AND MYSTICISM

Each of us, as a natural being, is growing both psychologically and spiritually at all times, even if we appear to be stagnant or stuck. Our experiences teach us continually just by their existence. In other words, we can't help but learn something about ourselves and our world in any life circumstance. We may appear to be going backwards, but all earthly experiences are for the purpose of catapulting us forward and will ultimately do so at the appropriate time. Psychological and spiritual growth cannot be separated, as we are psycho-spiritual beings. We are body, spirit, and mind, like it or not.

As opposed to religious growth, spiritual growth occurs *inside* us and may have nothing to do with ordained ritual or dogma. The most positive spiritual growth carries with it the awareness that we can help others and ourselves to the greatest extent by first transforming our own perception than by expecting or even desiring another to change. It is to understand that although we think we are limited or small, we are actually connected to and part of something much greater, more powerful, and more loving than we could ever suppose, and that to develop this loving part of us is the highest gift we could ever give to ourselves or anyone else. This includes the comprehension that change in relationships occurs whether or not both parties consciously choose to work on themselves. This is, again, because we are each connected to each other through our common link to the Divine Spirit within, and each of our attitudes, beliefs, and thoughts deeply affect one another.

Personally, I have witnessed many of my own relationships shift for the better just by doing my own inner work. I have watched countless couples, parents and children, co-workers and friends move from extreme conflict to respect and harmony in their interactions with one another because of their agreement to focus on their own inner issues, which needed to be addressed and healed. Positive spiritual growth occurs when we move into our loving hearts and out of our judgmental minds. It happens when we learn to forgive ourselves and others for being human and decide to treat all with honor and esteem. Constructive spiritual growth occurs when our own perceptions of what we see in ourselves and others shift and when we are able to see through our Divine eyes—the eyes of beloved affection.

To accomplish this, it is helpful to play the part of the mystic or the soul seeker. *Mysticism* is a much-abused word in today's world because it has become a catchall word for everything from crystal-gazing to tea-leaf reading. But *mysticism* in its purest sense represents the highest quest for human growth and awareness. The true definition of *mysticism* is the quest for the discovery of the ultimate self-reality. In other words, "Who am I, what am I doing here, where am I going, and where have I come from?"

Mysticism is the search for a Supreme Universal Intelligence that resides somewhere in the deeper levels of the human mind or consciousness. It is the attempt to make direct contact with this intelligence, to experience directly this presence, and to know that it can be contacted. The mystic follows the pursuit of *becoming aware of* the creativity and powerful aspects of this universal mind, in order to improve life for oneself and for all others. The mystically oriented soul seeker attempts to be intuitively guided by this intelligence in all facets of daily life, and continually works to integrate this spiritual force into all decision-making processes and creative work.

The more we grow spiritually, the happier and more peaceful we become, as we learn to relate to ourselves and others from a deep place of lovingness. To become mystically oriented means that we've chosen to seek our own truth and polish our behavior as a result of deep observation, listening, releasing negativity, communing with the Divine, and following our inner guidance. The rewards are nothing short of miraculous, for all we could hope for and wish for become not only a real possibility, but an eventual inevitability. Peace is ours to choose through the simple actions we take each day.

LEARNING THROUGH EXPERIENCE

A. *Explore these questions alone or with a partner:*

1. *How was I raised?*
2. *What do I believe about religion?*
3. *Do I practice any religion, and if so, how?*
4. *What kind of religious dogma lives inside of my mind?*
5. *Have I ever had a sensing of God's presence inside of me? If so, can I recall a time when that happened?*
6. *Have I ever noticed a change in one of my relationships because I myself made changes within? If so, what is an example of this? If not, what have I wanted to change in someone else?*
7. *If someone in my life changes because I want them to, will that make me happy? For how long? How much control do I have over other people's behavior? How much control do I have over my own?*

B. *Guided Meditation: Contacting Your Higher Self*

Allow yourself to relax, following your breath in and out ... in and out ... until you have left your outer world and have entered a profound, still space deep within. When the external world has quieted, and your concentration is centered within, imagine yourself to be in a very sacred place. It could be by a waterfall in the midst of a forest, it could be in a temple or church, in a field of flowers, or by the ocean. Anywhere you can feel free, peaceful, undisturbed by life's troubles ... Anywhere that heals your spirit. Let yourself be renewed in this place ... Let this be a place where you can receive any information you need to improve your life and the lives of those close to you.

Now, in the distance you see a ball of white light approaching you ever so slowly and gently. As it comes closer, it begins to change form, and you see a very wise, tender, powerful being emerge. This can take any shape you give it … an animal, a spirit guide, an appearance of light, a fairy goddess, a saint, or anything which carries with it the sense of wisdom, protection, and compassion. You may see it or sense it, hear it or feel it, but you know it's there, wanting to be of service to you. This is a higher part of you … a component of the fullest you, which exists at all times. Right now, this entity has entered your awareness to benefit you in some way.

As you sit with this being of wisdom, ask it how you can gain the courage you need to develop your most loving self … to rid yourself of any negativity that threatens your peace of mind … Ask it what your next step is … what you need to do in order to keep going, to let go, to move forward, or to have faith. As you breathe in, imagine that you are inhaling courage, strength, and wisdom into every cell of your body, your mind, and your soul. Feel yourself vibrating with bravery, with vigor, with might. You have become your higher self … you are one with God, with higher intelligence, with patience, kindness, and light.

Ask what you need to do to come to completion in any areas of your life which feel unfinished. Ask what direction to take … whom to contact … what to read … where to go … how to accomplish what you desire. Answers may or may not come immediately. You may sense rather than really know what to do right away. However, you may also hear very definite instructions. Don't worry if you don't hear anything right away. You are planting all the seeds necessary to attract understanding and direction. You ***will*** *receive answers at the appropriate time.*

Now, think about anything or everything you've come to know, sense, or feel in this meditation. Imagine planning today and tomorrow in a way that carries the energy you've experienced here out into your life. Recognize that this wiser, higher self is always a part of you … is always there to support you, guide you, and protect you. All you need to do is tap into it. Appreciate this part of you, and express your thanks for all you've heard, seen, or felt. Assure this higher self that you'll be back for more communion at another time, and know that you will always have this whenever you desire.

When you feel complete, very slowly open your eyes and come back into your external world … into the present moment. Remember for as long as you can, that you are more than your body and mind … you are a great being, loving, unlimited, and powerful. Come home to this thought and this knowingness … This is you!

C. *Prayers and Reflections*

Below are a few prayers or reflections I find helpful when attempting to commune with my higher self. Please feel free to substitute any vocabulary that might fit better for you. These have been worded in a manner that leads to communion with the infinite mind.

Psalm 23

You, God, are my shepherd: I shall not want.
You maketh me to lie down in green pastures;
You leadeth me beside the still waters. You restoreth my soul.
You leadeth me in the paths of righteousness.
Yea, though I walk through the valley of the shadow of death,
I will fear no evil, for you are with me;
Your rod and your staff, they comfort me.
You prepare a table before me in the presence of my enemies;
You anoint my head with oil; my cup overflows.
Surely goodness and mercy shall follow me all the days of my life;
And I shall dwell in your house forever.

Prayer of Saint Francis

Lord, make me an instrument of your peace.
Where there is hatred, let me sow love;
where there is injury, pardon;
where there is doubt, faith;
where there is despair, hope;
where there is darkness, light;
where there is sadness, joy;
O Divine Master, grant that I may not so much seek to
be consoled as to console,
to be understood as to understand;
to be loved as to love.
for it is in the giving that we receive;
it is in the pardoning that we are pardoned;
and it is in dying that we are born to eternal life.

Good Morning, Dear God

(anonymous)

Good morning, God. Thank you for this day—
a new, clean, fresh illumined day,
during which I can live and learn and love and give and grow.
I trust you utterly today
to pour your love through me all day long,
so that I have a plentiful supply
of strength, wisdom, and substance
to live every moment at its best.
I thank you for this gift of another day
in which to serve you.
Good morning, dear God.

Beloved, I am There

by James Dillet Freeman

Do you need Me? I am there.
You cannot see Me, yet I am the light you see by.
You cannot hear Me, yet I speak through your voice.
You cannot feel Me,
yet I am the power at work in your hands.

I am at work, though you do not understand My ways.
I am at work, though you do not recognize My works.
I am not strange visions. I am not mysteries.
Only in absolute stillness, beyond self,
can you know Me as I am,

and then but as a feeling and a faith.
Yet I am there. Yet I am here. Yet I answer.
When you need Me, I am there.
Even if you deny Me, I am there.
Even when you feel most alone, I am there.
Even in your fears, I am there. Even in your pain, I am there.
I am there when you pray and when you do not pray.
Though your faith in me is unsure,
My faith in you never wavers,
because I know you, because I love you.
Beloved, I am there.

Unity Prayer of Protection

Your light surrounds, me, God;
Your love enfolds me;
Your power protects me;
Your presence watches over me.
Wherever I am, You are.

Saying of Ramakrishna

The winds of grace are blowing all the time.
I have only to raise my sail.

Words of White Eagle

You are part of heaven. You are part of God. The whole Universe is the result of the impulse of love. God, the Supreme mind, the Divine mind, is all love. The main lifestream is love. Banish all thought of your disability. You, the Spirit, ***you*** *are the son or daughter of a living God, a power, a Divine intelligence; a great, loving, compassionate heart. You live and move and have your being in the Divine mind, the Infinite wisdom.*

By definition, Infinite Intelligence is perfect,
and thus the Universe and everything in it is perfect.
Human beings, as parts of the Universe are, therefore, perfect.
One of the hurdles that each of us must overcome
is to believe this.

—Arnold Patent

Chapter 3

How the Universe Works

AT a very young age, I began to take piano lessons. My father had taught himself to play when he was a teenager, and entertained us with his music ever since I could remember. His vision, of course, was that my two sisters and I would learn to play as well, so that we could reap the pleasures that such a beautiful and harmonic instrument might bring. As we were all musically inclined, it came naturally to want to perfect our skills at the piano bench. Thus began my endeavor to learn the art of piano playing. My parents could have taken me to an instructor who would teach me only how to read the music and transport the written musical notes to the keyboard, but they chose a teacher who believed that understanding music theory added tremendously to the process, and deepened one's ability to improvise, create, and perform. With an understanding of chords, musical symbols, and melodic harmony, the richness and breadth of our playing was augmented.

Just like the process of learning the piano, learning to cultivate love consciousness is an art and is enhanced greatly by knowledge of the workings of the Universe in which we live. While the world of music is the milieu for the sound of the piano, the Universe, with its unique characteristics, laws, and goals, is the backdrop for studying the art of loving. Understanding how the Universe operates can amplify our motivation, inspiration, and determination to open our hearts to love, even in the most challenging of times. So let's explore the nature of the cosmos, our true reality, in order to facilitate and intensify our skillfulness in this area.

ENERGY, THOUGHT, BELIEF, AND PERCEPTION

Everything in the Universe is made of an endless stream of *energy* and is part of an intelligence that is perfectly loving and all-knowing in nature. From the tiniest grains of sand and the smallest living organisms to massive buildings, mountains, and rocks, all is some form of energy, which, when seen under a microscope, is a vibrating composite of moving particles. Literally, anything we can think of that is seen or unseen is made of this intelligent energy. This means that there are energy forms that cannot be seen by the human eye but nevertheless exist. Radio waves or atmospheric gases might be used as examples of unseen energy. We know that one of the basic characteristics of energy is that *it cannot be destroyed.* It can change form, but it cannot disappear from existence. Therefore, anything that can be observed in some physical form is merely a transformation of something from nonphysical form.

How does something become visible then? This happens through the process of *thought.* Anything that is seen in the Universe has first been a thought in someone's mind. Just consider this. Before we had the lightbulb, Thomas Edison envisioned electricity and the mechanism to make light. Before we had the telephone, Alexander Graham Bell pictured the idea in his mind. The notion of the computer preceded its manifestation into the world of physical form. Therefore, we can see that ideas and thoughts are also a form of energy, and that our physical reality is merely thought transformed. Another way of saying this might be that our thoughts create whatever we see in our lives.

To take this a step further, not only do we create what we see with our thoughts, we also create what we feel and what we experience. Thoughts are powerful sources of creative and transformational energy, generating multi-faceted life conditions and feelings about them. Beliefs are learned thought forms, which are often unconscious, and can shape our quality of life for better or for worse. Beliefs are internal, often unconscious, decisions about the nature of reality. They have been imparted by our ancestors and society, and we have accepted them as truth whether they are accurate or not. Since we've been given free will by our Divine Source, we can choose any thoughts or beliefs we wish to have, and discard others. This puts us in a very powerful position, in that we can change our thoughts or beliefs anytime we dislike what we're feeling. Knowing this, we need only utilize awareness, patience, and persistence to develop greater mastery over our life circumstances.

A client of mine who had high blood pressure and heart problems awoke each morning with a feeling of dread at what the day would present to her. She had trouble getting out of bed and moving on with her day. Plagued by depression and fear, she would stay in bed and have to call in sick to work. Or, if she did manage to make it to her job, her day was filled with anxiety. Together, we explored her initial thoughts as she began to stir from sleep in the morning. When she shifted her thoughts from ideas such as, "I can't handle this," or "What if I'm hospitalized or die?" to, "I am strong and I *can* deal with this," her whole outlook changed, she was able to get dressed more easily, get to work, and even have an enjoyable day. Granted, this was not simply done, but with awareness of her thoughts, supplemented with determination and perseverance, over time, she was able to create a new quality of life. An extra bonus was that her uncomfortable physical symptoms decreased, and her health improved. With her fear weakened, she was more able to return to her loving nature, interacting with those around her in a fuller, kinder, and more peaceful way.

Perception occurs when our minds interpret what we have observed or experienced in such a manner that aligns with belief systems already unconsciously at work within our psyche. Because these belief systems are often hidden, we take them as truth and righteously defend them. They are frequently seen as factual, rather than perceptual, and, when negative in nature, they can cause great conflict within us and between us. If, for instance, I believe that my spouse doesn't love me because he spends so much time at work, I might feel anger, resentment, depression, or other negative emotions. Furthermore, I might not realize that this behavior is because of his strong desire to make sure that our family is financially secure, not because he doesn't love me. Yet, I might defend my position steadfastly, refusing to see the situation any differently.

In conclusion, we can see that we are each energy beings who are connected to an infinite river of consciousness or intelligence. We may appear to be just a body with a brain, but we are much more than that. We have manifested physically because of thought, and we carry that thought with us in the form of beliefs and perceptions. We are constantly creating feelings and life conditions, and can influence what we create by shifting them consciously. We are the designers of our lives and, in conjunction with God, hold jurisdiction over our inner experience.

UNIVERSAL LAW

Universal laws operate at all times and, when understood and upheld, hold the key to peace, happiness, and success. These principles are in place whether we like them or not, and whether we follow them or not. Unlike man-made laws, they are permanent and apply at all times and in all life situations. Because Infinite Intelligence governs the Universe, and because this intelligence is a purely loving energy, these laws are designed with our highest good in mind. Their ultimate purpose is to bring our minds into alignment with "God thinking" or love consciousness, which can only produce a sense of tranquility and freedom from strife. These may be new ways of thinking about the nature of the Universe for some, while for others, it is a confirmation of concepts already visited. Whatever the case, universal laws are merely a set of ancient truths that move us from conflict to peace. Again, belief in these principles requires an inner experience of their truths through practice, awareness, and contemplation. Therefore, I encourage you to try the exercises at the end of the chapter and pause in reflection for a moment after reading each of the following laws:

We Are All Connected by One Mind

There is only one mind in the Universe, and each of our minds is a part of this. We might call this mind Infinite Intelligence, or the God Mind, and there is actually no separation between what appears to be two different entities (me and it, or me and you). In order to experience happiness and lovingness, all we need to do is to tune into this part of our mind for wisdom, guidance, protection, and understanding.

Universal Abundance Is Our True Reality

At its core, the Universe consists of Divine energy, which is characterized by goodness and love. Therefore, the intention of the Universe is to supply everyone with exactly what they need. The result is that there is always plenty to go around, even though we often don't see it that way. Belief in lack is merely an illusion, or erroneous thinking. When we believe in lack, our thinking is not aligned with the God Mind; rather, it is aligned with the physical plane.

With a combination of education, attunement with Infinite Intelligence, and emotional expression and release, we can begin to see that we are indeed abundant. When we adopt a more satisfying belief system and let go of our fear of lack, not only do we create greater abundance in our lives, but we are also free to open our hearts to the love and peace that is always present.

Cause and Effect Are Continuously in Operation

This law is a reminder of what was discussed at the beginning of this chapter; namely, that each thought in the human mind causes the effect of something in the observable world. Whether we can actually see the effect, or whether we just sense it, we notice that it exists. By changing our thoughts (the cause), we can change the consequence (the effect). This provides us with the ability to influence the quality of our lives and offers a powerful tool in the creation of greater harmony for all.

Karmic Law Is Always at Work for Our Highest Good

Thoughts and actions travel in energetic form from our individual minds into the universal God Mind. Karmic law states that if these thoughts or actions are positive in nature, they will attract favorable life circumstances. If they are negative in nature, they will attract adverse conditions. Karma is *not* designed as punishment. To the contrary, Infinite Intelligence is loving and kind. Therefore, its intention is to teach us what produces peace and what triggers conflict. Its goal is to help us find and maintain a harmonious, happy, and untroubled existence. When conditions in our lives are unpleasant, we search for ways to alleviate our discomfort. Over time, we learn, through trial and error, what thoughts and behaviors work for our benefit and which ones cause detriment.

Everything, Except for the Goodness and Love of the Divine Mind, Is Impermanent

All conditions of life are impermanent except that of love. Love is eternal since it is the basic nature of the God Mind, and it can never be destroyed.

Anything other than this fundamental Divine state of mind is subject to change. Therefore, any negative circumstance of life is only temporary and serves the purpose of teaching some lesson about goodness and love. While in human form, the only certainty we have is that change will occur.

Because We Are All Connected, Giving Is Receiving

We've all heard the expression, What goes around comes around. This occurs because we are all joined by the God Mind. Others, therefore, are merely an extension of us, and there is nothing that we can do, think, or say that doesn't have an effect on the whole.

Whatever we give circulates back to us in some form. If we extend goodness, we will receive goodness. If we extend harm or negativity, we will receive the same.

SOUL LEARNING AND LIFE PURPOSE

Since energy cannot be destroyed, and because we are made of energy, we must assume that our essence lives on, even after the death of our body. What becomes of that energy, we can't be sure. However, according to Buddhism, we reside in other dimensions until we are ready to reincarnate into another body on the earth plane. Our energetic essence or soul, evolves throughout the entire process, so that through time, experience, and trial and error, the soul aligns its thought and belief systems with the God Mind. Eventually it knows only an existence of service, peace, and love.

During our residence in bodily form, we consist of what we might call the lower self and the higher self. The lower self is our personality, which does not yet see clearly through the eyes of compassion. In other words, it is the part of our mind that is not yet aligned with love-based consciousness or God-thinking. The higher self is the part of our mind that is filled with wisdom—the part that sees and understands truth, and knows what brings about a peaceful existence. We say that our world is one of duality, in which we often see ourselves as separate from others rather than joined as one. This is often true of our lower self. In such a state of mind we are in conflict within ourselves and with others. We may find ourselves deeply fearful, angry, lonely, or sad. This state of mind spawns war, domestic violence, drug abuse, and countless other adverse human situations.

If we explore the deeper questions of life such as, "Who am I?" "Why am I here?" or, "What is this existence all about?" we might come to understand that our lives actually have purpose. In my own search through years of education and inner investigation, I came to the conclusion that as souls, we are all here to learn lessons, just as we do in school. If we look upon our body as a learning vehicle and this earth plane as a school for our soul, we can see that our soul is learning to master the skills involved in loving. The more skillful we become, the more we create the inner peace that we long for, as well as peace between us and all other living beings.

If we look at life in terms of its lessons, how might we define the content of those lessons? In order to be fully loving and peaceful, we must develop attributes such as:

Acceptance	Harmonious Communication
Appreciation	Honesty
Balance	Hope
Charity	Honor
Compassion	Humility
Courage	Kindness
Empowerment	Letting Go
Faith	Patience
Forgiveness	Respect
Generosity	Surrender to Divine Will
Tolerance	

Think about this for a moment. Aren't these the very qualities we each seek to cultivate? If you contemplate your life history, you may find that there are one or more of these traits that you've been working on, and that the Universe has brought to you people and circumstances that could further your development. For instance, divorce may teach us to let go or to have faith, while remaining in a strained relationship may teach us harmonious communication, tolerance, honesty, or appreciation. Illness may teach us to develop greater balance in lifestyle, humility, patience, and courage. A critical boss might lead us to work on self-acceptance and empowerment, and raising a rebellious child might teach us greater respect, compassion, and again, patience. Once we release our anger, despair, or other negative emotions, we can go on to learn the greater lesson and see the higher good in what has happened. Any life situation can give us the opportunity to cultivate one or several of these traits. If we can see it that way, we are one step ahead of the game.

Most of us have been brought up to believe that we can make mistakes, or that we can fail, but when we see clearly, we realize that there is no such thing as a mistake, and no such thing as failure. There are only lessons. Through a process of experimentation, we learn what brings about peace and what creates disturbance. When we think we have failed, our suffering becomes as much a part of the process as when we perceive success. All life circumstances are our teachers, and sometimes the most difficult ones offer us the most in return. If we can see the gift in thorny life situations, and see such occasions as challenging rather than problematic, they may be easier for us to navigate.

It is important to mention that lessons are repeated until we have become highly skilled. We may think that we have gone through a particular situation before, and therefore, we shouldn't have to go through it again. However, there are degrees of learning. When we first learned to read, we may have said, "I know how to read!" But, in first grade do we read to the degree that we do in high school? Life lessons are the same. We may learn the lesson of generosity many times over in similar or different situations. And yet, we are always learning generosity to a higher degree each time. We may wish for a lesson to be over, but when we have mastered it, there will be a new lesson to learn. As long as our soul lives on Earth in a body, we will be learning lessons. Therefore, we might as well do our best to enjoy the process.

I have generally found in my life that whenever I travel through a very challenging period of time, it is followed by a less troubled and more relaxed interval of time. I remind myself that "spring always follows winter," so that I remember how loving the Universe is and that God does not desire that we suffer—only that we learn to be peaceful and happy. Holding these thoughts lends purpose to every life event and eases the pain of more trying ones. Infinite Intelligence bestows upon us whatever we need in order to grow, and it supplies us with the inner and outer resources to handle whatever comes our way. If we pay attention, tune into our inner guidance, and explore each life occurrence, we may find ourselves rejoicing in what we have learned and feeling more masterful over what used to knock us down. When this occurs, we find ourselves more compassionate, self-composed, appreciative, and content.

LEARNING THROUGH EXPERIENCE

A. *Take some time to contemplate answers to these questions, write your answers in a journal, or discuss with a partner:*

1. *What is one belief you hold that has created discontent or agitation in your life? What is one belief you hold that has created serenity or happiness in your life?*
2. *Think of something about your life that bothers you. What might be the thought(s) you hold that created this situation? What thought(s) do you suppose might produce a different result? What would that result be?*
3. *Think about someone with whom you have conflict. What is your perception of this person? Why do you think he/she behaves the way he/she does? What do you believe you factually know about this person? What do you believe you perceptually know about this person?*
4. *Have you ever felt connected to the One Mind? If so, when? Have you ever felt disconnected from the One Mind? If so, when? How did each feel? What is the difference between the two situations?*
5. *What do you believe about abundance? Do you think you have plenty or do you come from lack? Where do you think you got your beliefs?*
6. *What does karma mean to you? What feelings does it arouse? What are your beliefs about karma, if any?*
7. *What is an example of an impermanent condition in your life? What else is impermanent in your physical world? What do you believe is permanent, if anything?*
8. *Exercise: Imagine a situation in which you are quite angry and lash out at someone. What do you imagine might be the outcome*

of the situation for you—for the other person? How do you feel as you imagine this?

9. *Exercise: Visualize a situation in which you have volunteered to help out another person or animal who is needy. Picture what the situation is in full detail. See this person/animal in your mind's eye and imagine what you are doing. What might be the outcome of such a situation for this person/animal? For you?*
10. *What are the chief attributes you are learning in this life? Name three situations from your life that are teaching you these? Think about a life circumstance that is presently troubling you. What might you be learning from this?*

B. *We learn repeated lessons through trial and error. Read over the following poem by Portia Nelson, and, through reflection, explore any lessons you may have learned through a similar process.*

I.

I walk down the street.
There is a deep hole in the sidewalk.
I fall in.
I am lost … I am helpless.
It isn't my fault.
It takes me forever to find a way out.

II.

I walk down the same street.
There is a deep hole in the sidewalk.
I pretend I don't see it.
I fall in again.
I can't believe I am in the same place
but, it isn't my fault.
It still takes a long time to get out.

III.

I walk down the same street.
There is a hole in the sidewalk.
I see it is there.
I still fall in … it's a habit.
My eyes are open.
I know where I am.
I get out immediately.

IV.

I walk down the same street.
There is a deep hole in the sidewalk.
I walk around it.

V.

I walk down another street.

Falling down is inevitable; it's what we humans do.
When I acknowledge this, it brings me to an
unguarded kindness and sympathy.
Falling makes us human and
if such a thing can happen,
it makes us wise.

—Lin Jensen

CHAPTER 4

The Process of Growth

WHEN I was in my early twenties and beginning my search for solutions to my distress, I would embark on journey after journey thinking, "This will be the one!" Time after time, I seemed to find one philosophy, one mental tool, one book, one writer, one group, one therapist, or one idea that was going to end all my misery. I was convinced that the one answer was out there and all I had to do was find it. Needless to say, with that attitude, I was constantly frustrated, because whatever would work for a while would ultimately fall short of solving my entire puzzle. So I would continue my quest in the hope that next time I would find the magic cure. After thirty years of searching, I've discovered some powerful truths about the process of growth while perfecting the art of loving.

Specifically, I've learned that there are many answers and that growth is a complex and intricate process in which we glean a bit from here and a bit from there, and then move on to explore further. Furthermore, I've realized that the Universe, in its perfection, provides each of us with whatever our soul needs to evolve itself, and does so in a timely manner. This, of course, means that Infinite Intelligence has its own agenda, which does not necessarily correspond to the agenda set by our less wise lower self, who is often impatient, righteous, demanding, or needy. When these two agendas are in conflict, we can easily become discouraged, hopeless, anxious, or scared. Comfort is more easily found when we understand the principles governing evolution, the process of soul growth, and our connection to nature and this Universe.

EXPANSION AND CONTRACTION

The evolution of our soul and psyche is a process I call psycho-spiritual growth—*psycho,* meaning "of the mind," and *spiritual,* meaning "of the Spirit." The mind and spirit are inextricably intertwined, for as human beings, we consist of both. As we harness the power of the mind through repetition of experience, education, and practice, our soul evolves into greater perfection. This means that we possess a greater and greater ability to perceive everyone and everything through "Divine eyes," or love-based consciousness.

Most of us on a serious growth path would like to "be there yesterday." Emotional pain is uncomfortable and living life in fear-based consciousness can be quite difficult. Often, our worries, concerns, and hostilities can consume us, leaving us hopeless, dejected, furious, or sad. Other times, as we go about our daily affairs, a subtle anxiety underlies all that we do, even when we are quite functional and productive. We want to catapult forward and learn what we need to know, ASAP! However, growth is not like that. Evolution is never a straight path, but rather one of trials and tribulations, which bring us back on track to where we are going.

The evolutionary process is one of expansion and contraction, or being off course, then being on course. It is like climbing a sand dune, in that we can take two steps forward and then one back. We eventually get to the top of the sand dune, and with determination and persistence, we get there faster. Our steps backward inevitably occur, but they don't have to stop us from going where we desire. All souls become aligned with God-thinking eventually, for this process of expansion/contraction teaches us what we *do* want and what we *don't* want.

When we are in an expansion stage, generally we feel excited and joyous, or calm and peaceful. However, the contraction phase carries with it feelings of unease, agitation, or conflict. When our minds are unaligned with higher consciousness, we feel compelled to search for resolution to our discomfort. Therefore, we go on a search. For those who look outside of themselves to find relief, growth may become stalled, but those who realize that the answer can only be found inside grow more quickly and more surely toward their goal.

As you may notice in the diagram on page 68, we tread away from the path of love-based consciousness no matter where we are in our growth process. There is always more to learn, it seems, and the Universe, in its most loving but serious manner, lets us know that we have not perfected our thinking just yet. Our contraction away from the center line serves the purpose of demonstrating to us what kind of thinking and acting produces conflict. Our expansion toward the centerline reminds us of the power of loving thought and action to create happiness. The whole process is one of "forgetting" and "remembering." As we become more masterful, we will remember for longer and longer periods of time and forget for shorter intervals. With time, practice, and experience, we can retrain our minds to respond to all of life's circumstances with acceptance and a spirit of adventure. Living can become a fascinating voyage during which we expand our horizons and open ourselves to limitless possibilities.

Expansion & Contraction

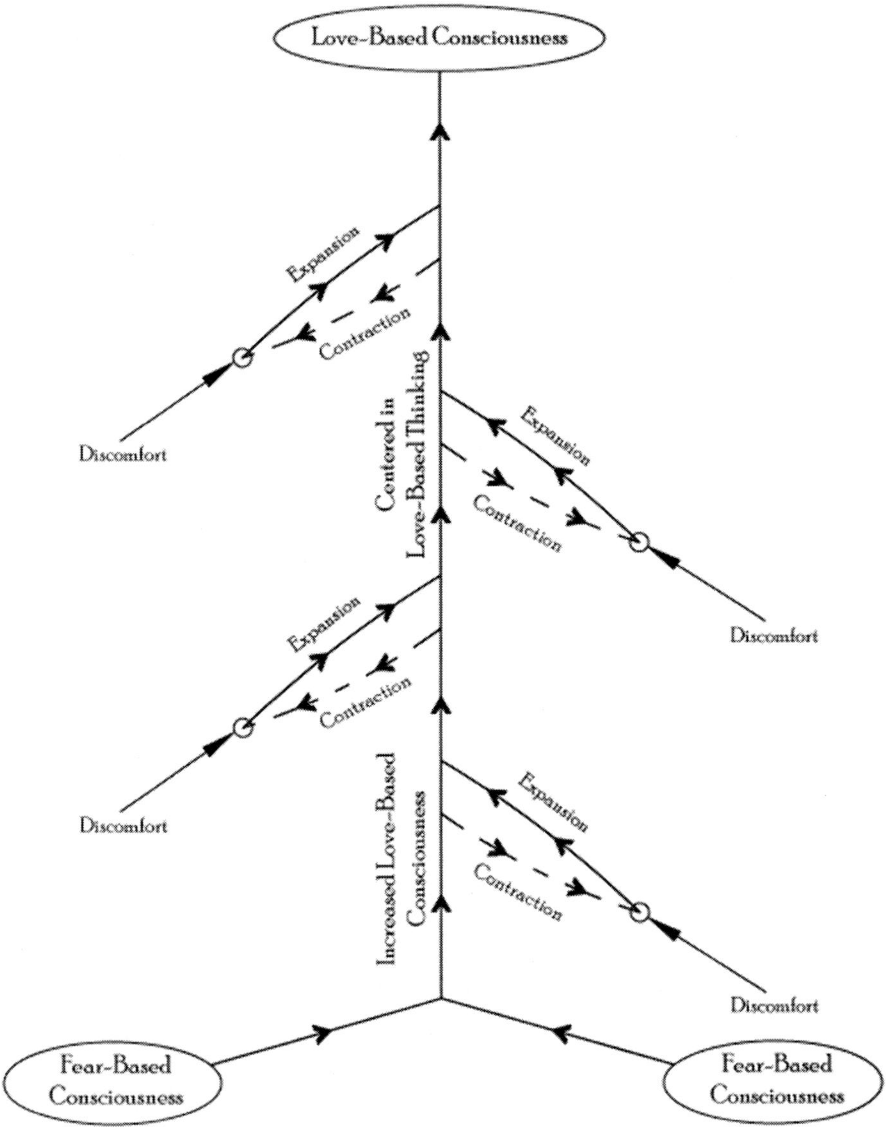

PEAKS, GULLIES, AND PLATEAUS

Another way to depict the growth process is to map out our journey in a manner that demonstrates what we will encounter along the way. When we look at our map piece by piece, we notice that, although we steadily climb our mountain toward love-based consciousness, we encounter peaks, gullies, and plateaus along the way, as seen in the diagram on page 70.

When our souls are young and immature (lower left corner), we have little or no mastery over life circumstances. We strive to find contentment and pleasure in the outside world, which brings only frustration or disappointment. In our discomfort we reach for knowledge to gain greater control over our feelings. During this time, we must release old emotional material, which is the product of our former life experiences. We also find that in order to gain greater peace of mind, we must become aware of what we are doing and thinking in order to make new conscious choices. This stage is a steep climb, which requires our energy, perseverance, and determination.

The good news is that at some point in our climb, the land levels out and we're rewarded for our hard work. Here we've reached a peak along our way. For the time being, we are free to rest and enjoy the view from this plateau of inner peace and calm. Throughout this time period, our psyche is stabilizing, absorbing the knowledge we've just gained on our upward ascent. Life is good (or better), and we have no major hurdles to clear.

When the Universe is satisfied that we've learned whatever was needed, it becomes time to move on to new lessons, and we find ourselves dropping into what I term as the gully. This is perhaps the most difficult terrain to navigate, for we may find ourselves in crisis or in deep emotional pain of some sort. Often we revisit old feelings of fear, anger, frustration, or desolation, and we wonder if we've made any progress at all. We are so uncomfortable that again, we seek answers to relieve our pain and find resolution, prompting us to climb once again.

Psycho-Spiritual Growth Process Model

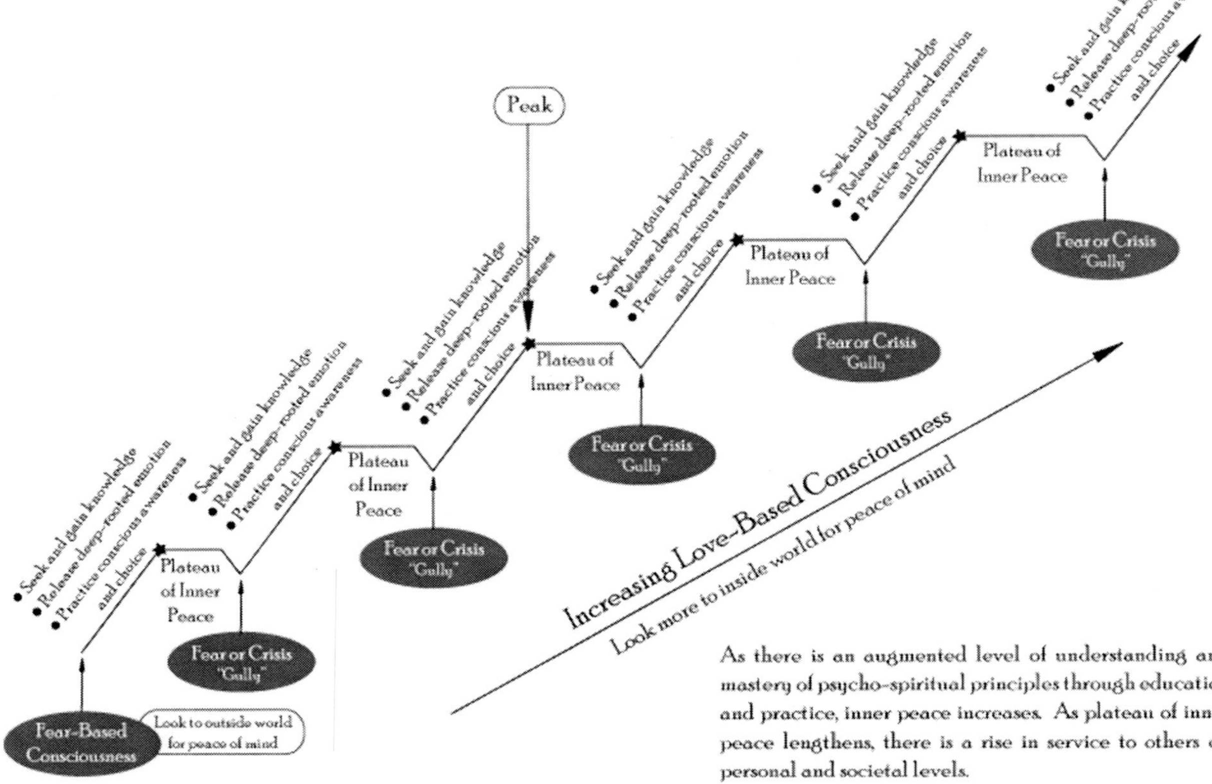

As there is an augmented level of understanding and mastery of psycho-spiritual principles through education and practice, inner peace increases. As plateau of inner peace lengthens, there is a rise in service to others on personal and societal levels.

For those of you who are consciously making efforts to grow and learn, this may make sense, and you may be able to identify with this process. However, I am often asked by students or clients about the many people they see in their lives who do not appear to be growing or changing in any way. Just remember that the growth that occurs during the evolutionary process of the soul is something that our minds often cannot fathom. It is a process that takes place over many lifetimes rather than during the timeline we have come to know as this life. Sometimes a gully can last a lifetime because the soul needs to experience discomfort for an extended period in order to learn a particular lesson. Other times the soul has contracted to learn only a small amount of material in this lifetime and the person appears to have an easy time of living. Just as we fluctuate with peaks, gullies, and plateaus in one lifetime, through eternity the soul's journey fluctuates as well, and this life span is all we are allowed to see at one time.

For those of you who seem to be on a steep learning curve, I call this being in the "winter of the soul." Often, one's experience in the gully could be referred to in the same way. It's good to keep in mind that spring always follows winter and that all conditions are temporary, as we have seen. If we attempt to be aware of what we are thinking, and if we are earnest and resolute about our search for truth and happiness, our winters will be shorter and often milder. We can then move on to our climb up the mountain and the inevitable plateaus of greater tranquility.

METAPHYSICAL SCIENCE AND GROWTH

While we dwell on this planet in bodily form, we are spiritual beings as well as physical beings of nature, sharing the earth with innumerable other life and nonlife forms. Ancient mystics and metaphysicians, wanting to understand their relationship to the Universe, studied the correlations between man and nature and between man and the spiritual realm. Arising, as a result of this exploration, were a number of metaphysical sciences or systems designed to aid human beings in their quest for greater ease of living.

These sciences were purely subjective in nature, as opposed to the objective or externally measurable sciences we learned about in school. They were ancient in origin, tracing back to early civilization, and were built upon observation and inner awareness. With media hype, some of these fields of knowledge have been perceived as ambiguous or controversial. However, with proper and careful usage, they can be beneficial to the growth process. When looking for a teacher in any of these areas, make certain this person is coming from a loving and ethical place and that the instruction feels intuitively right to you. Then personally test each theory to see if it seems relevant to your life.

Personally, I have found it advantageous to become familiar with some of these metaphysical systems, for understanding some of the principles involved has helped me to learn more about hope, acceptance, impermanence, letting go, patience, and more. Again, we can find truth only through our own experience of these bodies of knowledge. Therefore, although I present here a brief introduction to three of these fields of study, I urge you, if you wish, to pursue your own study and experimentation to discover whether the knowledge resonates within you.

As mentioned previously, as the soul evolves, the thought system of the lower self is becoming more aligned with that of the God Mind. Using the principles involved in these sciences, we may be able to facilitate this growth process by knowing what to focus on at a given time, what to avoid, when to slow down, when to speed up, when to make important decisions, and when to wait. Presented here are three metaphysical areas of interest you may find helpful during your growth process.

Astrology

Astrology investigates the influence of celestial bodies upon all living and nonliving material in our world and dates back to some of the earliest records of human culture. It is the forerunner of the science we now know as astronomy, and has intrigued mankind as a philosophy through its emphasis on harmony, symmetry, and wholeness. It is not to be used as a fortune-telling device, but rather as a tool for self-awareness and inspiration. Caution should be taken regarding limiting ourselves in any way because our chart reads in a certain way. We need always remember that we have been given free will by our Divine Source, and that success and happiness occur because of the choices we make every day.

With that said, the study of astrology can point out possible pitfalls and remedies, favorable times for working on particular tasks, and specific lessons we need to learn. It can help us to be less critical of ourselves, to see ourselves as ever-changing creatures connected to a greater Divine network, provide us with hope in troubled times, and aid us in developing endurance, patience, and persistence. In conclusion, exploration of astrological science can help us understand ourselves better, discover hidden attributes, and live a life of purpose, contentment, and productivity.

Numerology

The science of numerology, which predates Christ, is basically the study of numbers, their energetic vibrations, and their effect upon the material world. Its origins can be found in the Bible and in the writings of philosophers such as Pythagoras and Plato. Students of numerology regard it not as a religion but as a sacred body of knowledge, aligned with the teachings of all the great masters and sages of the ages. That is because its highest purpose is for man to understand himself and, therefore, perfect his ability to bring peace, success, and happiness to himself and to others.

According to this philosophy, each person possesses a particular vibratory nature determined by his/her date of birth and his/her name at birth. (Letters correspond to certain numbers.) In actuality, we are a conglomeration of several vibrations, depending on which numbers are added together.

Furthermore, each day, month, and year of our lives are characterized by a number from 1 to 9, each of which has a different nature. With this information, we can get to know ourselves in a new way, and understand where we are in our cycle of growth. For example, the number 1 represents new beginnings, or planting seeds. If we find ourselves in a year carrying the 1 vibration, we would not expect the fullness or completion of an undertaking to be found. Likewise, a month vibrating at 6 might be a time of great responsibility toward others, while that of 7 might be more introspective.

I find numerology to be valuable because it helps me maintain my awareness of a Divine plan, keeping me aligned with higher intelligence. How often do we long for things to be different from what they are? Numerology can help us accept life conditions as they are, while offering us guidelines governing our management of moment-to-moment affairs. The science presents us with constructive information about our character and what skills we are to be developing, leading us into greater harmony with our world.

Rosicrucian Cycles of Life

The Rosicrucians were an ancient metaphysical society of men and women dedicated to exploring inner wisdom and the meaning of life. Originating about one thousand years ago in Egypt, and then spreading to Europe and eventually to West, the teachings were passed down through the ages by scholarly, devoted, and masterful students. The Rosicrucian approach, through an understanding of cosmic and natural law, offers practical tools for living life with greater ease. Its purpose is to allow individuals to direct their own lives, experience inner peace, and serve humanity.

One of the Rosicrucian tools that I've found handy is their use of "life cycles," such that our year from birthday to birthday is divided into seven periods of approximately fifty-two days apiece. Each one contains different characteristics. By knowing the flavor of each period and how it might be used to its highest benefit, we develop patience, acceptance of change, hope, and greater mastery over our everyday life. For example, if I know that the seventh period of my year (the fifty-two days before my birthday) is a phase of less energy and contraction, I might be less concerned when a project I am working on is stalled. I can, at that point, understand that after my birthday during period number one, everything may fall into place due to this phase's more expansive and vigorous nature. With such knowledge, we can allow ourselves to flow more with the ups and downs of life, aligning ourselves with the rhythmic harmony of our earthly existence.

LEARNING THROUGH EXPERIENCE

A. *Think about the following questions and talk about them with a trusted friend. Continue your journal writing if inwardly directed.*

1. *Reflect upon your growth process. Recall one or more occasions during which you experienced an expansion phase. Remember one or more occasions during which you experienced a contraction phase.*
2. *Contemplate your growth over the last five years. See if you can find occasions when your growth peaked, when you leveled out into a plateau of greater peace and calm, and when you experienced the gully.*
3. *Think about your life. What did you know five years ago … ten years ago … twenty years ago … thirty years ago? How did you deal with life challenges at each of these times?*

B. *Take a few moments to ponder the following quotes and apply them to your life and to the lives of one or two significant others.*

The truth is that our finest moments are most likely to occur when we are feeling deeply uncomfortable, unhappy, or unfulfilled. For it is only in such moments, propelled by our discomfort, that we are likely to step out of our ruts and start searching for different ways or truer answers.

—M. Scott Peck

It's not so much that we're afraid of change
or so in love with the old ways, but it's
that place in between that we fear …
It's like being between trapezes. It's Linus
when his blanket is in the dryer.
There's nothing to hold on to.

—Marillyn Ferguson

To exist is to change, to change is to mature,
to mature is to go on creating oneself
endlessly.

—Henri Bergson

Whosoever wishes to know about the world
must learn about it in its particular details.
Knowledge is not intelligence.
In searching for the truth, be ready
for the unexpected.
Change alone is unchanging.
The same road goes both up and down.
The beginning of the circle is also its end.
Not I, but the world says it: all is one.
And yet everything comes in season.

—Heraklietos of Ephesos

If there is right in the soul,
There will be beauty in the person.
If there is beauty in the person,
There will be harmony in the home.
If there is harmony in the home,
There will be order in the nation.
If there is order in the nation,
There will be peace in the world.

—Lao-Tzu, Chinese philosopher

CHAPTER 5

Inner and Outer Peace

WORLD PEACE BEGINS WITHIN

OUR world, as we know it, is in trouble. No one debates that. Not only are nations at war with each other, we are often at war with our family members, co-workers, friends, and neighbors. Our natural resources appear to be dwindling, our air and water are poisoned with pollutants, extinction of many species of wildlife is a real possibility, and poverty invades two thirds of our planet. Some people remain angry about job loss or are frozen in fear at the prospect of not being able to feed their families, while others move through life in a constant state of anxiety or hopelessness. Some resort to drugs, alcohol, shopping, or overwork, while others point their finger at all those responsible for their problems.

What can we do, we ask? Our congressmen, senators, and other government officials desperately seek answers to the call of distress, and many of us perform acts promoting social welfare. But we still look around us and, as one problem improves, another worsens. War still occurs, even after experiencing its horrors time and again. As a human culture, we seem to be lost. We look to change everyone and everything else—to find solutions in the outside world, for, we tell ourselves, there surely must be an answer out there. We just haven't found it yet.

And, yes, there is an answer, but the ultimate answer is not to be found where we have been looking. It is to be found only inside of each of us. It may seem, at the moment, that we have no clue as to how to fix the world, but to the contrary, human consciousness has been moving forward and upward for a long time, and we are fortunate to be living at a time during which the ground has already been prepared for a great leap in awareness. This jump forward allows us to see that the answers were always inside of us. We just had to look inward to find them.

At the heart of every system, be it a family, a business, a government agency, a legal-judicial system, a health care system, or even a collection of systems, such as what forms our world system, we find that the system is built upon the mind-set of each and every person within it. Personal healing of our attitudes and our perceptions, therefore, evokes transformation within the system. We have the power to transform virtually every cultural system through education and the willingness to look at ourselves with keen observation, express and release our feelings in a healthy way, and hold ourselves in compassion. Once we find peace inside of ourselves, we automatically extend it out into the world, for peace and love cannot be contained; they must be shared. Our higher selves know this truth; at our core, we strive to connect lovingly with each other and, when we're centered in a tender, caring place, we cannot be stopped.

The wonderful thing about healing our minds and our hearts is that our love becomes contagious. When one person responds to life in a loving and peaceful manner, everyone he or she touches, benefits. When someone refuses to be drawn into a fight, but rather, chooses to see the goodness in everyone involved, he models Divine behavior for others. If we hold fast to loving vision, others will follow suit, even if it takes many tries. Human beings all desire peace. Through healing our own hearts and minds, we demonstrate possibility and give permission to others to work on healing as well.

World peace seems evasive. Most likely we won't be able to see it in our lifetime. However, like all evolutionary processes, establishing peace on earth calls upon each world citizen to evolve individually in order to affect the whole. The part that each of us plays is not insignificant, as some of us may believe. Since love is the strongest and most powerful healing force in existence, and because we are each capable of bringing love into play, we have within us the potential to heal the world. Every small stride we take toward realizing our unity and our perfection possesses this healing power and has an immense effect upon all with whom we come into contact as well as those we don't even know. We can each make a difference just by doing our own inner work.

The more loving we become, the more the events of the planet reflect that love. To truly love means to care about and respect all facets of nature, including animals, people, plants, trees, oceans, and the air we breathe. To truly care means that we view everyone and everything as a precious creation of God, and that we go about our daily life with this attitude. Yes, we each have the power to affect change in this world. Inner peace *is equal to* outer peace—world peace begins within.

PERCEPTION AND ITS CONSEQUENCES

When my two sons were in elementary and middle school, I worked as a counselor in a clinic. Because many clients were unable to attend sessions during the day, I would often work in the late afternoons and evenings. When I would finally arrive home, our house would be in total disarray—toys, shoes, papers, socks, jackets absolutely everywhere! At these times, I would often lose my patience, become angry, and yell at my boys. Needless to say, they would then become even more unruly and begin fighting with each other and with me.

In those chaotic moments, I learned to step back and examine my perceptions of what I saw. Eventually, after some thought, I came to the realization that my anger was induced by my perception that my kids were naughty and disobedient and that I was a bad mother for not teaching them correctly. The real truth was that my boys were oblivious to the mess and were having a great time playing together. They were just boys being boys and exuberantly enjoying life! They had merely forgotten what I had taught them about cleaning up.

I found that I had to work on healing my perceptions in order to create peace in my house. With time and patience, I learned to respond to their antics in a firm but calm way. I also learned that empathy and forgiveness went a long way toward convincing them to listen to my requests. In addition, I saw that recognizing myself as a good and loving mother (my natural core), were the necessary ingredients to maintaining my calm and therefore, a peaceful environment.

Our inner perceptions, as mentioned previously, create the atmosphere of wherever we find ourselves. Let's suppose you were raised to believe that money is hard to get and that you would never have enough of it. Perhaps that is what your parents believed and taught you to believe through their example. As an adult you marry and have children, but you're always living in fear of not being able to support them properly. The energy emanating from your mind literally tells the Universe that this is the way it is. The consequence of this is that the Universe brings to you situations that reflect this mind-set. One day, you lose your job, as the company for which you work downsizes. This triggers your sense of yourself as a failure, which perception you also learned from your parents and from a culture that may equate job loss with lack of success. Now you go home in a rotten mood, fight with your spouse and kids, and then withdraw into a shell. The next day, your wife, feeling quite low herself, snaps at the clerk in the grocery store and ignores her children's pleas for attention. Now the children begin to act out at school. And so it goes, like ripples in a pond. Multiple others are affected and conflict spreads like wildfire. Perception has consequences. It has the power to create peace or discord.

World poverty is caused by similar perceptions on the part of many individuals. Lack is a mind-set to which there is vast agreement. The original cause of war is a perception on the part of those involved that people are either good or evil or behave correctly or incorrectly. Abuse may occur because one falsely believes that they are unlovable or faulty. One may be a victim of abuse for the same reasons. Perceptions are often unconscious, but they rule our planet. Each perception has a consequence that sets off a chain of events.

When the perceptual system of the human race has significantly been altered to reflect its all-loving and all-accepting nature, the world will be a different place. When we realize that we are all part of the wholeness of creation and that we each deserve to be honored as such, the world we see now will no longer exist. When we realize that there is no such thing as failure or evil or faulty character, but just soul lessons, our Earth will be a place of peace, plenty, and purity.

SERVICE

As the soul evolves, triggering our memory of our true nature, we find ourselves opening to compassion and service. According to universal law, love is a force that cannot remain still. The very nature of love is to be active and to seek places to expend its energy. The more peaceful we become, the more we want to share that peace with others. Personal growth is not a selfish endeavor. Its ultimate purpose is help the whole, of which we are all a part.

In the words of White Eagle, master, author, and teacher:

*If you endeavor to raise the Christ**
within you, you help to raise all humankind.
You cannot make one effort toward
heaven without the whole of the world, even
the very earth itself, being the better for it.

*Christ, in this sense, refers to love-consciousness.

Because love is the core energy of the Universe, all earthly experiences occur in order to bring a greater quality of service to the world. Whatever you might be going through, it is merely a preparation for the eventual assistance you will provide later when you are ready. The world as we know it, seeks our healing for purposes that might be hidden from view right now. And yet, if we keep on keeping on, day by day, and moment by moment, we eventually will arrive at a place where we must give what we have gotten.

When I was in my teens, twenties, and thirties, struggling to work through my anger and fear, I often found myself withdrawn and introspective. I felt guilty that I was not actively engaged in community service or some helping profession. At times I even lacked the energy to reach out to family and friends. However, the inner work I accomplished at that time was a stepping-stone to my future. Without it, I wouldn't have been able to significantly affect the lives of the people I've assisted in the past twenty years. The God-Force was laying the groundwork for me to serve in my own unique way.

Over the years, I've observed numerous clients, students, and friends prepare themselves for unknown future service. One client who was sexually abused as a child found herself years later working as a social worker with abused children and their families. Another, in dealing with food addiction, found the tools she needed to later assist others who struggled with cravings and compulsions. Another had taken yoga classes while grappling with the stress of being a college basketball coach. Years later she became the owner of a yoga studio where she could offer others her administrative skills as well as her knowledge of yoga and its benefits.

Service is not confined to the helping professions. Consider the boy who is born and raised in Africa but moves to this country as a teenager when his father takes a new job. The images he received as a child live in his heart and, as an adult, he is moved to raise money to help the poverty-stricken in Africa, although his chosen profession is that of a boxer. Then there is the woman who was abandoned by her own mother but is determined that her own daughter will never suffer alone. When her daughter ends up in a nearly fatal car accident, the mother, for months, rarely leaves her side until she is well enough to resume her life.

There is no experience wasted in the Universe. All has meaning and purpose. As we heal mentally and spiritually, we are each called upon to serve the whole in an innumerable number of ways. As we gain peaceful wholeness inside, our natural urgings to bestow good upon this world become stronger, our desire to share our learning with one another increases, and our ability to effect change rises. The more we choose to heal our hearts, shifting ourselves into a more peaceful place, the more powerful our effect is on the whole. In order to realize the alleviation of the world's ills, all we have to do is look inward and do our own work. All else follows automatically.

LEARNING THROUGH EXPERIENCE

A. *Take some time to contemplate these questions:*

1. *How committed are you to finding inner peace, on a scale from 1–10? What might block you from being committed at a 10 level?*
2. *Think of one time when you looked to your outside world to find your peace. Where did you look? Did you find it? Could you count on this again and again?*
3. *What kind of inner healing work have you done? How successful have you felt? What's your next step?*
4. *Do you become angry at or fearful of the world situation? How do you deal with your feelings? How might you choose to see this differently with what you now know?*
5. *Think of a time when you reacted in anger. What were your perceptions of the situation—and of yourself—in the situation? According to what you've learned so far, how might you shift these perceptions to create more peace and harmony?*
6. *Think of a time when you reacted in fear? What were your perceptions of the situation and of yourself in the situation? According to what you've learned so far, how might you shift these perceptions to create more peace and harmony?*
7. *When have you been of service to someone else? How did it feel? When have you been of service to yourself? How did it feel?*

B. *Prayers for Healing: Inside and Outside:*

From the depths of holy silence, I give
thanks for the joy and energy of life.
May all beings enjoy the vitality
of their existence.

I remember all who suffer great pain and
long-term illness. May the Healer of Hurts
breathe balm and restoration into all
wounded lives.

May all negative, angry, and harmful
attitudes that I harbor within me
be transformed into new and
available life.

The dance of a Summer day calls my
steps: may I respond to the rhythm
and melody of its music.

—Caitlin Matthews

O Lord,
Open my eyes that I may see the needs of others
Open my ears that I may hear their cries;
Open my heart so that they need not be without succor.

Let me not be afraid to defend the weak because
of the anger of the strong, nor afraid to
defend the poor because of the anger of the rich.

Show me where love and hope and faith are needed,
and use me to bring them to those places.

And so open my eyes and my ears
that I may this coming day be able to do some
work of peace for thee.

—Alan Paton

May we learn to open in love
so all the doors and windows
of our bodies swing wide
on their rusty hinges.

May we learn to give ourselves
with both hands, to lift
each other on our shoulders,
to carry one another along.

May holiness move in us
so we pay attention to its small
voice and honor its light
in each other.

—Dawna Markova

Lead us from death to life,
from falsehood to truth.
Lead us from despair to hope,
from fear to trust.
Let peace fill our hearts,
our world, our Universe.

Let us dream together,
pray together,
work together,
to build one world
of peace and justice for all.

—Anonymous

Dear God,
We pray for this our world.
We ask that You remove the walls that separate us
and the chains that hold us down.
Use us to create a new world on earth, one that
reflects Your will, Your vision, Your peace.
In this moment, we recognize the power You
have given us to create anew the world we want.

Today's world, dear Lord, but reflects our past confusion.
Now, in this moment, we ask for new light.
Illumine our minds.
Use us, dear Lord, as never before, as part of a
great and mighty plan for the healing of this world.
May we no longer be at war with each other.
May we no longer be at war within ourselves …

Remove from our hearts the illusion that we are separate.
May every nation and every people and every color
and every religion find at last the one heartbeat we share,
Through You, our common Father/Mother and the
redeemer of our broken dreams. May we not hold on to yesterday.
May we not obscure Your vision of tomorrow
but rather may You flood our hearts.

Flow through us, work through us, that in our lives
we might see the illuminated world. Create, sustain that world
on earth, dear God, for us and for our children. Hallelujah, at the
thought. Praise God, the possibility that
such a thing could come to be, through You,
through Your light that shines within us.
So may it be.
So may it be.
We thank You, Lord. Amen.

—Marianne Williamson

I asked God for strength that I might achieve,
I was made weak, that I might learn humbly to obey.
I asked for health, that I might do greater things,
I was given infirmity, that I might do better things.
I asked for riches, that I might be happy,
I was given poverty, that I might be wise.
I asked for power, that I might have the praise of men,
I was given weakness, that I might feel the need of God.
I asked for all things, that I might enjoy life,
I was given life, that I might enjoy all things.
I got nothing I asked for, but everything I hoped for.
Almost despite myself, my unspoken prayers were answered.
I am among all men, Most richly blessed.

—prayer by unknown Confederate soldier

CHAPTER 6

Adversity

TWENTY-three years ago when my first-born child was two years old, I collapsed from fatigue and "nervousness." I had been in school working on my master's degree, while, at the same time, I was experiencing the wonders, trials, and tribulations of being a new mother. While many mothers are capable of handling that amount of stress, for some reason, I was not, and my body broke down, sending me into a cycle of fear that is unforgettable. How would I care for this child? How would I finish my degree? What would everyone think? How weak I would look! Maybe I was dying!

At the time, I felt swallowed up and paralyzed by my fear, unable to function to any reasonable degree. The world seemed to be moving around me, and yet I remained in a cocoon of anxiety and depression. I left my son with my husband and sought refuge in the home in which I was raised, spending much time alone and attempting to rest for a few weeks. While this occurred, there arose a wiser part of me that knew I needed to face my apprehensions no matter how terrifying they might be. Much as I wouldn't have consciously chosen to be in that state of emotional and physical exhaustion, my higher self told me it was a necessary part of my journey toward inner peace. And so, like it or not, I found myself reaching for answers, for a new way to frame my experience in my mind, and new ways to perceive myself and my world.

Over time, I learned many lessons about living with adversity and the magnificent gifts that could be obtained by walking through stormy weather in a conscious and trusting fashion. Of course, this wasn't always easy to do, especially when I found myself in great pain. Learning the arts of loving and peacefulness, I found, are often difficult. For many of us, the process of getting there is a path lined with prickly bushes, slippery spots, and potholes. Adversity seems to peek its head out at each corner, often challenging us to our very core, as it did to me at that time of my life.

As I have since learned, the first noble truth of Buddhism is that all beings suffer to one degree or another. For those seeking spiritual wisdom or greater enlightenment, the road can be quite treacherous, as the desire to "see" more clearly draws forth circumstances that transform the inner, lower self. This may involve experiences that bring us to our knees or situations that cause us to look deeply inside of ourselves. We may feel forced to spend time alone or to seek therapists and teachers who can help us mend and transform ourselves. That is what I was required to do at the time of my illness, and I spent many months rediscovering parts of myself that had been quite hidden from view.

Those parts of me were merely pockets of built-up fear that had never been resolved and were coming up to the surface to be seen, handled, and released. In having asked for and committed myself to opening my heart to love, I drew to myself the very conditions that would unblock me. No matter how I might seemingly resist those experiences, my soul had already pledged itself to peace and love. I had just forgotten and needed to be reminded. During my time of illness, I felt weak, incapable, and terrified, but as I began to heal, I also realized that the only way to get back on a "God" track was to confront my fears and move through them, which I found to be quite possible, with time and effort. I found out that even though fear itself can be multifaceted and multilayered, healing even one of those layers could be freeing and could also be the source of feelings of triumph and accomplishment.

As I journeyed through those months, I became less afraid of pain, illness, and death, more compassionate toward others who suffered, stronger in my resolve to contribute to the world in some way, and more courageous in tackling hardship. I also saw that I hadn't been true to myself in pursuing my real interests because I was afraid of what my family and friends would think of me. I learned to follow my heart no matter what others might say about me and to allow myself to embark upon a metaphysical voyage that might be ridiculed or judged to be hogwash. All of those lessons, of course, were complex and continue to this day, but during that time of intense adversity, I made great strides in changing belief systems that until then had only obstructed my vision and hindered my ability to be the kind, calm, compassionate person I was designed to be.

ADVERSITY AND FAITH

Faith, in a spiritual sense, is belief in and devotion to a God-Force in the absence of logical, tangible, or material proof. In the many years I've been working with clients, I've noticed that when I've asked about their degree of faith, many mention that they believe in God or a higher power, but are either angry with God, unsure of God's powers, or afraid of God. This confirms the notion that fear-based consciousness has educated many of us in an erroneous manner, and that there is a much more favorable way to view this God-Force, as mentioned in previous chapters. This is to understand that Universal Intelligence is total goodness and love. If given a chance, the Divine will back us in any endeavor and in all circumstances. The Universe is concerned only about our highest good and is present to assist us in creating the peacefulness we crave. It is not the Divine's wish that we experience adversity. Rather, it is God's desire that we remember our own divinity and realize in our hearts and minds that we are safe and will always be protected. This, to me, is the true test of faith and can be learned only through experience.

Since it is God's wish that we understand the fallacy of fear, we are brought circumstances that test and develop our faith. When I was in the beginning stages of my illness, my conception of the God-Force was confusing, at best. I did know there was a higher power, based upon my miraculous pregnancy described in chapter 2. However, in my life at that time, I had seldom experienced that extraordinary power. I was a neophyte in recognizing the Divine working on my behalf. I needed experiences that drew me inward to prayer, meditation, and contemplation, in order to realize the amazing power of God's love. The Universe obliged.

In my darkness, I was humbled, falling to my knees over and over again in entreaty. I needed help navigating my way through the shadowy tunnels of fear and gloom. With much prayer, emotional release, and finally, greater acceptance of my condition, it dawned on me that I was being exquisitely nurtured each step of the way. A teacher here, a book there, a friend's words, a spiritual passage just right for the moment, a doctor, a therapist—it was all there when I needed it. All I had to do was ask. Over time, I was developing a safety net and learning that I really had nothing to fear at all. With my new understanding, I was able to see more clearly that the God-Force, which lived within my being, was my protector, my true salvation, and the lyrics of "Amazing Grace," "I was lost but now I'm found," finally made sense to me.

When we're faced with difficult conditions, we must first ask ourselves what this adversity is all about. What is it trying to teach us? What fears is it helping us to overcome? Do we have fears of physical illness or pain? Do we fear losing a loved one or being alone? How about the fear of failure, rejection, ridicule, or poverty? Realizing that we can relinquish all of these fears and put faith in their place is the greatest antidote to adversity. Hardship can be our friend rather than our enemy. When we can see the good that is emerging from a situation, when we can develop the foresight to see where a situation is taking us, we begin to drape the prickly bushes with fur, we fill in and smooth over the potholes, and we melt the ice on slippery spots. Harsh conditions become gentler and, although our tears may still flow or we may shake still with anxiety, we recognize that we are cleansing out old worries and frights, ones that do not serve us any longer and from which we will soon find freedom.

Adversity need not rip us apart. It is our road to happiness, completeness, comfort, and peace. If we are willing to weather the storms that pass through our lives and call upon the Divine power of the Universe as our strength and sustenance at those times, we will surely conquer our greatest fears, experience glorious victory, and emerge with confidence, sparkle, and joy.

THE SPIRITUAL WARRIOR

To transform oneself requires an enormous amount of energy, drive, and determination. It is necessary oftentimes to stay the course, even when voices within are screaming at us to turn around and retreat into familiar territory. Such is the case for soldiers in the wars of our world, which are merely a manifestation of the inner wars we fight as humans. When we are caught in a difficult situation, we are called upon to develop our strength, our courage, and our perseverance. We are sometimes asked to work through inner issues that threaten to consume and destroy us. We are frequently forced to fight as though we are warriors engaging in battle.

Being a spiritual warrior is giving it all we've got, and when we fall down, getting right back up and continuing on. A spiritual warrior understands that inner thought systems must be changed and obsolete belief systems discarded in order to see truth and then act from a higher, more evolved space. A spiritual warrior aims to benefit others through laboring internally for the acquisition of inner and outer peace.

Many of us have earlier memories of times when we faced adversity and had no useful tools to handle what confronted us. Those times may have been full of upset and pain. The world through our eyes may have seemed full of gloom and doubt and, having no guidance at the time, we may have been unable to change the way we felt. Therefore, we come into new hardship with old programming that says, "I can't handle this. Life is miserable, and it hurts too much." The greater truth is, we may not have learned just yet that we *can* be strong and courageous. Each of us has that innate ability because we are of Divine nature.

The place to begin conducting ourselves as spiritual warriors is in our minds. We start by examining our thoughts. What are we saying to ourselves? Remember that our thoughts create our reality. Consequently, if we are thinking that we can't cope and that life is sad and depressing, that is what we will create—a life situation full of weakness and unhappiness. On the other hand, if we mentally affirm that we *can* cope with this, and that we intend to bring joy and peace into our lives, the means to produce this will unfold. It doesn't matter if we believe it or not. If we say those words *as though* we believe them, that is what we will create.

As we work at changing our negative thoughts to positive ones, we can rest assured that the Universe will take care of the rest. As spiritual warriors, we exercise patience, practice, and determination, returning to the job even after falling down. This means that whenever we can be conscious enough to note our thoughts, we make an effort to stay positive. If that effort falls short, which it will at times, we learn from the consequences and move on without judging ourselves.

Of course, there may be times of great resistance. We must remember that our past is loaded with experiences, during which we acted in destructive ways. The past is also laden with old emotions we neither understood nor expressed very well. Making changes in our lives requires the release of these old feelings and thoughts so that calming new perceptions can dawn in our consciousness.

Release occurs in many ways, no one way better than another. We can release on the spiritual, emotional, or physical planes. Discharge on the spiritual plane is a release of energy occurring as thoughts, pictures, or words in our minds. On the emotional plane, we can cry, scream, weep, throw temper tantrums, or merely talk to let go of what no longer serves us. Physically, we shake, have diarrhea, get colds and flu bugs, or our skin erupts with stored toxins. Physically, there is a multitude of ways our bodies discharge what they longer need or want. Most inner transformation occurs on all three planes at one point in time or another.

Spiritual warriors face all this during times of great stress, crisis, or difficulty. They move back and forth between release of old toxic material and working with existing thought and belief systems. The result is a reeducation of the mind and the heart. It is a continuous journey of throwing off the old and taking in the new. It can be a tough process but one well worth the effort.

During my breakdown, there were times when I felt lost in confusion and felt as though I were going nowhere. There were moments when I had no idea what to do next. When I learned new tools for handling my crisis, I would use them diligently only to be frustrated by the lack of manifestation of what I wanted to see happen quickly. I would experience distress over and over again before I would gradually begin to see the light. I developed the endurance and perseverance of the spiritual warrior because my intent was to heal and learn from my experience. I refused to give up because I knew inside that I needed to become more empowered and courageous in my approach to life. These are the trademarks of the spiritual warrior. Adversity offers us the perfect opportunity to use the power inside of us to march forward into the land of love-based consciousness and to cultivate the skills necessary to get there.

THE WOUNDED HEALER

Great adversity often spawns the ability to be present with others in an enormously compassionate and insightful way. Someone who has been through his or her own storms possesses the skills and capacity to help others through similar hardships. Even if the circumstances are not exactly the same, the wounded healer has developed an understanding of the nature of pain for living beings.

If I had not experienced my own life difficulties, I would be acting from my head and not my heart when called upon to counsel clients or come to the aid of friends and family in trouble. To be able to feel someone's anguish as though it were your own is one of the most significant keys to being with someone's wounded soul and assisting in their healing process. During my illness, I remember originally working with a therapist who had no idea what I was going through. Although she tried to help me, I didn't feel understood or genuinely cared about. I left her rather quickly and continued my search for someone who could comprehend the depth of my emotion and could share their own battles and victories with me. My greatest healing took place later with several different teachers and friends who had already undergone related circumstances and who could share their stories and their triumphs.

I've noticed that those who've suffered through divorce and learned from the experience are often the most helpful to others who are struggling with the breakup of a marriage, a business, a family, or a partnership. Those who've undergone job loss are the most effective source of aid to those grappling with the harsh realities of attempting to support a family while out of work. Individuals who've lost a spouse or a child are frequently the greatest source of comfort for grieving widows, widowers, and parents. These people are particularly helpful and can be classified as wounded healers if they've suffered deeply and come through their ordeal to a point of triumph, insight, and empathetic understanding.

Every adversity is for the ultimate purpose of preparing us to serve others in love. The wounded healer understands this and cherishes the gifts that have come out of his/her own distressing life events. Universal Intelligence is perfect in the sense that it always utilizes the abilities of wounded healers to contribute to the well-being of the whole by bringing together those needing help with those who can offer it. The ultimate goals of the Universe are always for our highest good, so that we may release fear and experience peace. The benevolence of the God-Force can be felt when we have pulled through difficult circumstances and moved on to help others in need.

Thus, adversity can be seen as a strengthener. If we allow ourselves to learn from hardship by looking for purpose in the midst of difficulty, we can develop greater faith, courage, stamina, insight, and compassion. We cannot mold the will of the Universe to fit what we think we want or need, but if we are persistent and optimistic, nurturing our patience and committing ourselves to inner growth, we will awaken one morning to the sound of music, to the fullness of our hearts, and to the bright manifestation of our dreams coming true.

LEARNING THROUGH EXPERIENCE

A. *Spend some time contemplating the following. As usual, answers may be discussed with others or written down in a journal.*

1. *List three of the most difficult times of your life on the left side of a piece of paper. On the right side, think about and write down the various lessons learned from each circumstance. What abilities were you developing during each instance?*
2. *Contemplate an adverse situation from your past. At the present moment, do you consider your experience worthwhile? If so, why? If not, why not?*
3. *How would you rate your faith in the God-Force on a scale from 1–10? Why? How might you increase your faith?*
4. *Have you ever viewed yourself as a spiritual warrior? If so, when and why? What traits do you need to develop to improve your ability to be a spiritual warrior? How might you work on this? If you don't know, what might be your next step?*
5. *Who do you know that demonstrates great strength and perseverance? Talk with that person and ask her how she developed these characteristics. Ask her to share some difficult life experience with you and tell you how she managed to get through it.*
6. *Who do you know who might be a wounded healer? What is this person like? Why would you consider him to be a healer? When have you seen him in action?*
7. *Might you be a wounded healer? If so, why? When have you helped someone else through hardship? How effective were you?*

B. *In times of trouble, contemplate the following and examine your feelings and thoughts as you read the words:*

What if the situations in my life that seem to bring up the most fear and frustration and grief come in love's service?

What if they're all opportunities to wake me up from the trance of my fears and my belief in separation?

I am given circumstances I require for my awakening. Every situation seen rightly contains the seeds of my freedom.

Darkness and fear are the great awakeners. In facing my demons, my fears, I will find my freedom.

—Joan Borysenko

It is the wind and the rain, O God, the cold and the storms that make this earth of Thine to blossom and bear its fruit. So in our lives it is storm and stress and hurt and suffering that make real men and women bring the world's work to its highest perfection. Let us learn then in these growing years to respect the harder, sterner aspects of life together with its joy and laughter, and to weave them all into the great web which hangs holy to the Lord.

—W. E. B. Du Bois

Do you need Me? I am there.
Only in absolute stillness, beyond self,
Can you know Me as I am,
And then but as a feeling and a faith.
Yet, I am there. Yet I am here. Yet I answer.

When you need Me, I am there.
Even if you deny Me, I am there.
Even when you feel most alone, I am there.
Even in your fears, I am there
Even in your pain, I am there.

I am there when you pray and when you do not pray.
Though your faith in Me is unsure,
My faith in you never wavers,
Because I know you, because I love you.
Beloved, I am there."

—James Dillet Freeman

I am not weak, but strong.
I am not helpless, but all powerful.
I am not limited, but unlimited.
I am not doubtful, but certain.
Dr. Paul Masters

When one door of happiness closes, another door opens; but often we look so long at the closed door that we do not see the one that has been opened for us.

Difficulties meet us at every turn. They are the accompaniment of life. Out of pain grow the violets of patience and sweetness. The richness of human experience would lose something of rewarding joy if there were no limitations to overcome.

—Helen Keller

C. *Guided Meditation*

Find a place to sit in silence and breathe comfortably for a few minutes. Make sure you won't be disturbed by the telephone or other noise for ten to twenty minutes. Allow yourself to relax into a space of calm, clear awareness, noting the way you have felt today and contemplating any difficulties you might be facing right now.

Now, transport yourself to a very peaceful place, somewhere that is beautiful and serene, where the energy warms your body and your soul with its greenery, its openness or its loveliness. Perhaps you are on a mountain top, or in a field of lilies, or on a beach at sunrise. Maybe you're in the woods or on a tropical island or in a room with walls and comfortable chairs covered in purple velvet. Allow yourself to choose exactly the right spot for yourself where you can slow down, unwind, and loosen up. Continue to breathe for a few minutes.

When you're sufficiently relaxed, bring your attention deeply inside of you to your heart center. Be aware that in the heart center lies the source of your most powerful and loving self. This is the wise self that knows all and cares only to protect and nurture you for all the days of your life here on earth. Allow yourself to feel this love now. Let the white light of love enfold you in its embrace as it fills each and every cell within your body and mind. The light drapes over you, adorning you in all its glory and tenderness. Feel it … experience it … sense it …

Now, taking this cloak of light with you, allow your present difficulties to come to mind. What are you afraid of? Visualize your fear. What does it look like? What color is it? What is its texture?

Put the fear in front of you and let it speak to you. What does it want you to know? Let it express itself until it feels finished. Feel any feel-

ings that may come up in the process. Allow yourself to cry, scream or shake if you feel the urge. Let it all out—release it and be with it.

Now, remember the wise, loving self you found inside your heart center. Once again, permit the light to envelop you and then to speak. What does your wise self say to your fear? Let it talk softly, gently, affectionately. Allow it to calm your fear with words your fear needs to hear. Take time to do this. Be patient and allow the words to come naturally. You need not force anything. Note any changes in the way you feel. If there are no changes and you hear no words, rest assured that you have been heard. If you practice this meditation over and over again and/or discuss your experience with a person you trust, you will resolve the issue and diminish your fear.

As you end your meditation, envision yourself wearing your cloak of glowing white light as you come back into the outside world. Remember that you can call upon this energy at any time and soothe yourself through its benevolent and bountiful power.

You learn to speak by speaking,
to study by studying,
to run by running,
to work by working;
and just so,
you learn to love by loving.
All those who think to learn in
any other way deceive themselves.
—Saint Frances De Sales

CHAPTER 7

Conscious Choice

LONG ago, as I was growing up, I often perceived life to be scary and many people to be unfriendly. Because there were high demands placed upon me in terms of what was acceptable or unacceptable behavior, I frequently felt that I was living on pins and needles, afraid to speak my truth for fear of being criticized. I had little understanding of my family members, let alone myself, and reacted to life from a repertoire of automated mental responses. I felt that I had no choice. That was the way life was and I had to submit to it. I hated myself for being so powerless, and I resented my family members, for I believed that they *made* me powerless.

As I journeyed through my growth process, I came to realize that I had attracted these family members to me because they were my greatest teachers, and that because I was so uncomfortable in this environment, I would be impelled to change my attitudes. In other words, there was a great deal I could learn in this living situation, one of the most important lessons being that I had choices. Choices were available to me in all sorts of shapes and sizes: choices about how to think, what to say, how I wanted to react, how I could perceive my family members and myself, and choices about how to view life itself. I hadn't known that, and my lack of awareness gave rise to suffering miserably.

As human beings, we have been given free choice by a loving Universe. I've found that the questions we must ask ourselves are: What are our choices, and what are the consequences of each choice?

Because we've grown up in a world where fear-based consciousness is so pervasive, many of us are unaware of what our choices are. We've been educated in such a way as to be programmed in fear-based thinking and therefore, we often robotically respond to life in an "attack, defend, or retreat" manner, which is so common in our society. To fit in and avoid rejection or ridicule, we stop questioning our responses and do what's familiar and seemingly safe, even though it refuses to bring us happiness or peace. The age-old statement, "ignorance is bliss," is erroneous where self-awareness is concerned, for it offers us what appears to be the easiest way, and yet lacks any possibility of real resolution.

To discover and utilize new choices requires education and introspection. If we don't know what the new choices are, we can't use them. Therefore, we must first educate ourselves, whether by reading, taking classes, hearing speakers, working with psychotherapists, watching videos, listening to tapes, or observing peaceful people whom we emulate. Next, through mindful awareness, we must apply our learning to our inner life (thoughts and feelings), experimenting with new responses, releasing blocked emotions, and finally consciously choosing how we want to think and behave. It is through conscious choice that we can create freedom from anguish and peace in the face of difficulty. It is with conscious choice that we can break the generational cycles of fear-based thought and plant the seeds of love for the future of the world.

WILLINGNESS AND MOTIVATION

Letting go of old, automated responses and choosing new ones can take a great deal of effort. Our lives are busy. Often, we're either working, taking care of children, going to school, running errands, helping out family members and friends, tending to our homes, or engaging in myriad other activities for which we're responsible. Understandably, carving out time for inner transformation is not exactly a high priority on everyone's list. Motivating ourselves to take the time to work with our thoughts and feelings can be a real challenge.

In addition, self examination is often hard work, requiring us to look at parts of ourselves we would rather not see—the parts of ourselves that we keep well hidden from view because we dislike them. Change may mean that we must let go of friends or relationships that we've outgrown. We may feel a sense of emptiness in that we don't fit in anymore with groups to which we've belonged, and it may take awhile to find new ones that feel right. In other words, at times, self-growth can be a rather challenging process.

For those reasons, it is often difficult to motivate ourselves to do the work. Fortunately for us, the Universe loves us so much that it wants nothing less than pure happiness for us. Therefore, in its infinite intelligence, the Universe provides us with situations that cause us to suffer enough discomfort that we may feel "forced" to grow toward greater peacefulness. That is how evolution operates, as you might recall from chapter 4. If we are passive and hide from ourselves, waiting for the Universe to push us, the pain we experience may be worse than the pain we feel if we allow ourselves to consciously choose to work on inner transformation. If we keep on hiding in spite of our discomfort, we may experience serious disease both mentally and physically. If we consciously commit ourselves to the process, however, our "gullies" may be shallower and our climb less severe. Even if we struggle through our growth process or live with disease, we will reap the incredible rewards of our labor by experiencing periods of grace, gratitude, and wisdom known only to those on a conscious path.

What is meant by consciously committing to the process? First of all, it is the willingness to prioritize personal growth in spite of our busy life styles. This might suggest that we put aside fifteen to thirty minutes a day for reading, contemplation, prayer, or meditation. It might imply that we sign up for a class we've been meaning to take, or make an appointment with someone to discuss different ways to view our life challenges. It might also mean going to church, synagogue, mosque, ashram, or other places of worship more frequently or spending more time in silent awareness. The point is that we must place ourselves in an environment conducive to introspection and exploration on some sort of a regular basis. How much time we spend on this is a very individual decision.

Second, *consciously committing* to the process is the willingness to do our inner work in spite of any discomfort we might experience on the journey. It is often said that if we have the willingness of a mustard seed, God will do the rest. When we keep in mind that the rewards of such work are peace of mind, decreased conflict in our relationships, greater faith, connection, compassion, and appreciation, then it is easier to be willing.

Willingness and self-motivation are conscious choices that we make for happiness. We can wait until the choice becomes a desperate one, or we can act now, saving ourselves from greater misery. We hold freedom of choice over when and how to proceed on our evolutionary journey. Thus, we have the power to do it now rather than later—today rather than tomorrow. The world needs our love and our goodness right at this moment! Why wait?

HOW THE MIND WORKS

While exploring conscious choice, it is often helpful to understand the makeup of the mind so that we have an idea of how we might better utilize this extraordinary instrument, which is our natural inheritance. Using Penney Peirce's model of the mind from *The Intuitive Way,* we can see in the diagram on page 110 that the mind is composed of three parts, the superconscious mind, the subconscious mind, and the conscious mind. My own interpretation of this model follows.

The Superconscious Mind

The superconscious mind is the part of the mind that is joined with all other minds and makes up the largest percentage of the mind, approximately 85 percent. It is the branch of the mind that is in touch with Infinite Intelligence, Divine Spirit, pure love, compassion, understanding, and wisdom. It is from that source that we experience our most loving selves and think in ways that are cooperative, harmonious, creative, courageous, caring, and respectful.

Our soul receives its knowledge directly from this part of the mind and because of this, our soul knows what lessons we need and adopts a lesson plan for our learning while in physical form. The soul, in conjunction with the guidance of the Greater Divine Spirit, picks its parents, body, and life circumstances.

The Subconscious Mind

The subconscious mind is the part of the mind that holds our memory bank of experiences. Included in this storage system are memories of emotionally charged past soul experiences from this life and others. This is a reservoir of fear, blame, conflict, and suffering and is well hidden from view unless we consciously choose to uncover and observe the contents.

Parts of the Mind

Superconscious Mind
Infinite Intelligence
Spirit
Soul

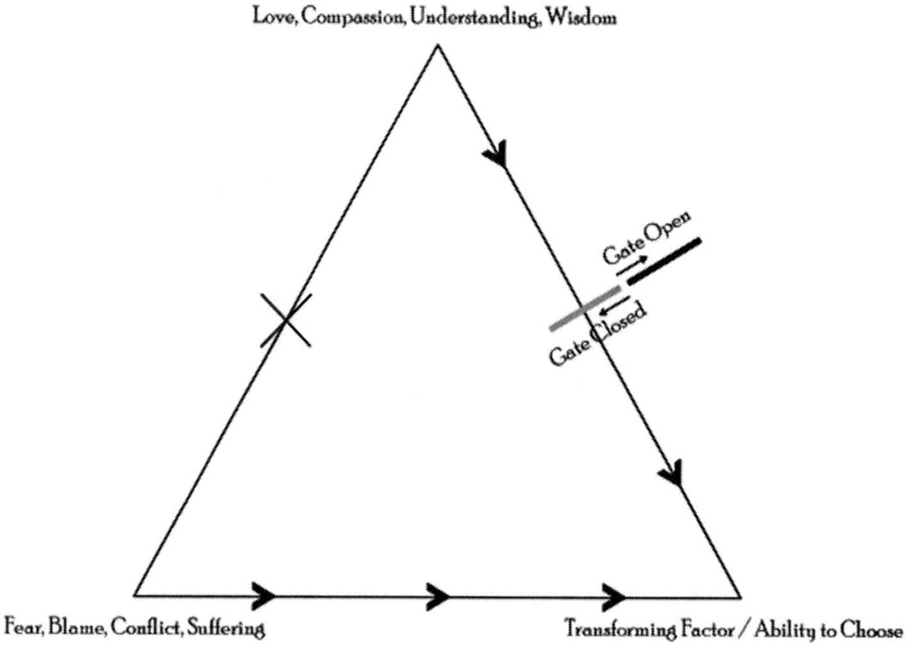

Subconscious Mind
Ego
Memory Bank

Conscious Mind
Will
Choice

A Course in Miracles labels this part of our mind as the ego, and states that we are separate and alone in the world; that is, we are disconnected from the God-Force. When we operate from our ego, we blame others for our suffering and believe that our distress is because of something someone else did, not because of our inner perceptions and beliefs. Consequently, we relinquish our power to the outside world instead of recognizing that our true power lies inside of us.

The Conscious Mind

The conscious mind is the part of the mind that is capable of observing and transforming automated, habitual responses. Awareness is its main feature, coupled with its ability to utilize will to make new choices. The conscious mind observes everything that comes through our senses after it has filtered through the subconscious mind and the superconscious material available to us at that moment. It then has the ability to choose to act from either place.

As we refer to the diagram on the opposite page, we can see that there is a continuous flow of material from the subconscious mind to the conscious mind. This accounts for the frequency of our reactive, habitual, behavior. The more emotionally charged material we have stored in the subconscious mind, the greater the occurrence of fear-based reactions to life situations.

However, there is also a river of wisdom, love, and compassion attempting to flow toward the conscious mind at all times. We can *use conscious choice* to open or close the gate to this superconscious realm of knowledge. Activities such as prayer, contemplation, meditation, positive affirmations, mindfulness, spiritual reading, gratitude, expression of feelings, and acceptance open the gate to the superconscious mind and its valuable contents. Each of these will be covered in chapter 8.

As can be seen, there is no communication between the superconscious mind and the subconscious mind. We interact with the world around us only through the conscious mind, which is fed by the other two streams of thought energy. Therefore, we can readily comprehend the enormous significance of the conscious mind, which carries with it immense possibilities for creating peace through its ability to consciously choose our reality.

THE CHOICE FOR COMPASSION

Peace is ultimately created through compassion, even though it isn't always an easy choice. When we feel angry or hurt, it's difficult sometimes to deal with our feelings, let alone put them aside and choose compassion. We may need to express and release our feelings in a therapeutic manner before we're ready to look at ourselves or others empathetically. We may need to talk about our feelings with a trusted individual or seek to understand another's behavior prior to the selection of compassion. However, it helps to set our intention in that direction, as intention carries with it a powerful energy to create.

Compassion contains the understanding that, as human beings, we are all doing the best we can with what we know and with what we've been taught. Most of us are a product of some sort of fear-based consciousness, mainly because this is the thought system of much of our world. That means we've been raised to criticize or evaluate ourselves and others, to compete for money, grades, attention, and the like, and to judge everyone and everything as good, bad, or somewhere in between. We're afraid of failure, sometimes of success, of rejection, and of being alone. We're fearful of being fired or laid off, ill health, life, and death, etc. These fears block us from being the compassionate individuals that we naturally are. Wars between nations and conflict among family members and friends occur because we've forgotten how to be compassionate toward each other, that is, to put ourselves in the other guy's shoes. In addition, we feel that if others don't do it, why should we?

The choice for compassion is a gift we give ourselves as well as others. Inner peace is the product of extending ourselves in a loving way. We can't truly be happy and serene unless we offer what it is that we want. That is because, as you might remember, a basic law of the niverse is that whatever we give out circulates back to us in some form. Thus, we must ask ourselves what stands in the way of our choosing compassion and how might we go about resolving this problem.

In terms of our triangle denoting the three parts of the mind, compassion flows from the superconscious to the conscious mind. Fear and anger flow from the subconscious mind to the conscious mind. If we can allow our conscious mind to bathe in an ocean of love, understanding, and wisdom emanating from the superconscious mind, the negativity of the subconscious will eventually dissolve, leaving us with an easier choice for compassion. That is because love is the supreme healer and, in its presence, everything else melts away. Therefore, learning to keep the gate open to Infinite Intelligence is of paramount importance and can be the very catalyst needed for compassionate responses to stressful situations.

The choice for compassion is always available to us and it transforms us from assuming a reactive stance to life to adopting an active one no matter who, or what, we're dealing with. It puts the power back in our hands and can determine the extent of our happiness and the happiness of others. The choice for compassion, understanding, and love is what will eventually heal our Earth and all of its inhabitants. It is a way of giving back to the very nature that spawned us, and of helping to harmonize our planet. Seeing the world through the eyes of those with whom we share it and offering understanding and honor, emboldens us all to live a creative, joyful, and united existence, no matter how diverse we may seem. The choice for compassion is simply one of the most powerful choices we hold and warrants our deep consideration.

LEARNING THROUGH EXPERIENCE

A. *Explore the following questions and activities alone or with a trusted friend:*

1. *Think of a time when you responded to a situation in an attack, defend, or retreat manner. Imagine how you might have used conscious choice to respond differently. What might you have done instead?*
2. *How many alternatives to attack, defend, or retreat can you think of?*
3. *How much time do you spend on inner transformation and/or consciously examining your automated responses to life? How might you motivate yourself to do more of this?*
4. *Specifically, what do you do to work on your personal growth? Is there anything more you feel inwardly guided to do?*
5. *Name one recent thing you said, did, or thought that emanated from your subconscious mind … your superconscious mind … your conscious mind?*
6. *Spend a day (or an hour) observing your thoughts and actions. On a piece of paper draw lines to make three columns. Label one column "subconscious mind." Label the second one "superconscious mind," and the thir, "conscious mind." Assign and record as many thoughts and actions as you can to their corresponding category.*
7. *Spend a day thinking about responding only compassionately toward others. How easy or difficult is this for you? Notice the consequences. How does it feel to do this?*

B. Contemplate the following passages.

Attitude

The longer I live, the more I realize the impact of attitude on life. Attitude, to me, is more important than the past, than education, than failures, than successes, than what other people think or say or do. It is more important than appearance, giftedness, or skill. It will make or break a company ... a church ... a home. The remarkable thing is we have a choice every day regarding the attitude we will embrace for that day. We cannot change our past ... we cannot change the fact that people will act a certain way. We cannot change the inevitable. The only thing we can do is play on the one string we have, and that is our attitude ... I am convinced that life is 10 percent what happens to me and 90 percent how I react to it. And so it is with you ... we are in charge of our attitudes.

—Charles Swindoll

An Indian Tale

An old Cherokee is telling his grandson about a fight that is going on inside him. He says it is between two wolves. One is evil: anger, envy, sorrow, regret, greed, arrogance, self-pity, guilt, resentment, inferiority, lies, false pride, superiority, and ego ...

The other is good: joy, peace, love, hope, serenity, humility, kindness, benevolence, empathy, generosity, truth, compassion, and faith ...

The grandson thinks about it for awhile and then asks his grandfather, "Which wolf wins?"

The old Cherokee simply replies, "The one I feed."

—author unknown

C. *The following concepts are taken from A Gift of Peace, Selections from A Course in Miracles, edited by Frances Vaughan, PhD and Roger Walsh, MD, PhD. Consider what this means to you and how it applies to your life.*

The Choice for Peace

Each choice we make is a decision for or against peace.
Each of us has the power to make this choice.

This world can change through us. No other means can
save it, for we are the lights of the world.

Therefore, choose and choose again, and let us make our
choice for all our brothers, knowing they are one with us.

There is an ancient peace we carry in our hearts and have
not lost. Peace is the natural heritage of Spirit.

We are free to refuse to accept our inheritance, but we
are not free to establish what our inheritance is.

Peace and understanding, strength and innocence are not
in conflict, but naturally live in peace.

Let us lay down our arms, and come without defense into
the quiet place where heaven's peace holds all things still at last.

Let us lay down all thoughts of danger, fear, and attack,
for here lies true strength where no weakness can enter.

If we look with peace upon our brothers, God will come rushing into our hearts in gratitude for our gift.

If we want the peace of God to pervade this world,
We must choose love and choose love again.

Only then will we find God's eternal peace,
And this world will be healed.

Whenever you are asked
if you can do a job,
tell 'em, "Certainly I can!"
Then get busy and find out
how to do it.
—Theodore Roosevelt

CHAPTER 8

Tools of the Trade

IN the many years I've counseled clients and students, I've noticed that most of them report that they're suffering in some way and would like to be more peaceful and content, but they have no idea how to get there. Discomfort has prompted them to look for a toolbox whose contents can provide them with the means for filling their emptiness and bringing more love into their lives—the inner ingredients for happiness.

As a young adult, I too, lacked such a toolbox, for I had never received an education in the arts of love, harmony, happiness, and peace. It wasn't taught formally in either religious school or grade school, perhaps because teachers and administrators, educational planners and government officials struggled with the same issues and therefore prioritized other academic curriculum. Maybe it was too difficult to teach what was not fully understood. I also witnessed fear-based activity in the news, at home, at school, and between friends. My role models were inconsistent at exhibiting unconditional love-based behavior, just as most of us are.

Nevertheless, in my own search for inner and outer peace, I've discovered a number of tools designed to open our hearts to fullness and love and aimed at developing the tranquility for which we all long. As you may recall, each of these tools helps us to open the gate to the superconscious mind, allowing the flow of wisdom, compassion, and understanding to be uninterrupted as it proceeds toward our conscious awareness. Here, we will examine some of the tools available to us as we continue our journey toward peace.

SPIRITUAL READING/LISTENING/EDUCATION

Long before I knew what I know now, I coped with life in the best way I could, but was often filled with uneasiness, frustration, and discontent. During the breakdown period of my early thirties, I felt guided to read. I read every spiritual book I could get my hands on, for I was hungry for knowledge—hungry for a new way of seeing everything in my existence—in this world. Reading others' stories and experiences helped to ease my pain and taught me how to interact with life in a manner that was novel to me at that time. I was given ideas and exercises that, after a while, became a part of me and transformed or augmented my inner knowing.

Since that time, spiritually oriented books, tapes and CDs have become my friends and constant companions. They offer me connectedness and allow me the opportunity to contemplate new choices, activities, philosophies, and belief systems. Through time, I've gleaned from them what works for me and secured a personal view of the kind of life I want to live. Therefore, I've included a bibliography in the back of this book with some of the book titles of the material that has held meaning for me over the years.

With that said, there is the challenge of finding time to read, particularly for those of us who work full time and have family commitments. In these cases, I often suggest listening to audio material while driving, as long as it doesn't interfere with one's concentration on the road. Each of us must consider whether this would work safely for us. In addition, some clients inform me that they are slow readers or find reading tiring or boring. That has been the case for me at times. When this is true, I frequently suggest that a book need not be read from cover to cover. Sometimes all that is needed is a page or two to lift our minds into a higher more thoughtful realm, away from the busy hustle and bustle of daily life.

In addition to spiritually oriented reading and listening, there are classes, workshops, conferences, seminars, and groups to join. These are places to meet like-minded people and to take in new education. There was an extended period of time when I was like a sponge, soaking in all kinds of new mystically oriented thoughts and experiences, and I felt the need to find appropriate instructors to help me sort through it all. Holistic shops, bookstores, and newspapers are a great source of information about where to find out what's going on around you. Churches, synagogues, mosques, or ashrams frequently offer such events. The keys to choosing the correct ones for you are the following:

1. Ask yourself if it *feels* right to you on the inside. Go because you want to be there and you're curious about it, not because someone else thinks you ought to.

2. Make sure that once you've entered a class, workshop, or seminar, that the energy emanating from it is loving and that there are no expectations of you as a student coming from the instructor or figures of authority. In other words, make sure that whatever you choose to do with the class material is your decision, not someone else's. Love allows freedom of choice without force. It is your right to opt whether to stay or leave.

PRAYER

When I was small, I prayed every night with all my heart, asking God to bless everyone I personally knew and those I didn't know who might be suffering. This nightly ritual was an important part of my life until I was about ten years old. By that time, I had experienced deep depression and, although I had been including myself in my prayers, I felt that God had abandoned me, and I wondered if prayer did any good. In my teen years, I gave up my practice, thinking it wasn't helping anyway. It wasn't until I was twenty-nine that prayer came back into my life, this time with full force. As you may recall, I began praying around the time I became pregnant with my first child. Because conception was a dramatic demonstration of God's existence for me, I began to pray again in earnest and have continued the practice for nearly thirty years. However, that first insightful moment has evolved over time into a more thorough appreciation of the nature of prayer and its miraculous power.

Prayer is a practice that many of us use only when we're pushed up against a wall and don't know what else to do. Fortunately, this uplifting tool can be utilized anywhere and anytime with valuable results. The key, I believe, is to understand the workings of prayer and what elements give prayer its greatest power. While it is clear that prayer involves an energy output from the conscious mind to the Universal Mind, what ingredients cause our gate to open and remain open, so that only good can reach our awareness and our happiness can be ensured?

I've discovered the following helpful hints that can keep us aligned with Universal purpose.

Let Go of the Outcome

Whenever we pray, we usually have something specific in mind that we want. When we attach ourselves to a specific outcome, we can set ourselves up for disappointment and disillusionment if we don't get exactly what we've asked for. We must remember that the will of the Universe is always for good and that whatever happens occurs for the highest benefit of all those involved. Trusting the God-Force isn't always easy, but if we're persistent with our prayer, we'll eventually find ourselves embraced by some miracle, even though it might not be precisely what we originally requested.

Example:
Oh, Great Spirit, Please allow my ailing father to live longer so that he might participate in his family's lives and receive the joy that this brings to him. If it is his time to go, may you keep him comfortable and give all of us the strength to handle whatever happens. Please help us to accept your will, knowing it will generate the highest good for our whole family. Thank you so much.

Include Others in Your Prayer Desires

We are all connected and part of the whole. Infinite Intelligence always has this in mind when receiving our prayers. If our prayers are self-centered in nature, we will still be heard and answered in some way. However, to add power to the effect of our prayer, it is helpful to include how what *we* want will benefit *others* as well. It is as though the Universe sees that we are in alignment with its goals and therefore hastens to satisfy the wish. Anytime we are in alignment with love, we open the gate to superconscious involvement. We are actually inviting our lives to be flooded with Divine assistance.

Example:
Oh, Loving Lord, I ask today that you guide me to find a teacher, therapist, or friend who will help me to make peace with my past so that I might be free of the inner turmoil I am experiencing. I know that if I am able to get beyond this pain, I will be better able to show love and kindness to all I know and meet, particularly my family, my co-workers, and

my friends. Help me to be of greater service and to let go of this anguish. Thank you for your love and support.

Be Specific Without Attaching to the Outcome

Prayers are composed of thought energy, which travels into the Universe and triggers a particular response based upon the content and vibrations of that energy. Sometimes when we are too vague with prayer, The God-Mind is unaware of what we really want. Often, we end up getting only a version of what we originally set out to find. By being specific, we ensure that we will attract whatever circumstances we need to create the manifestation of our desires.

It is useful to be aware that the manifestation of our longing may involve several stages. We may ask for one thing, but we are not yet prepared to receive it. The Universe must provide us with the step-by-step requirements for materialization of our original request. If this is the case, it is beneficial to be persistent in our prayer and not give up just because we don't see our exact request manifested. Continued prayer effort always takes us in the direction of our specific desires.

Example:
(Weak) Divine God/Goddess of the Universe, please send me a soulmate.

(Powerful) Divine God/Goddess of the Universe, please send me a loving, supportive, nurturing man/woman with whom I can share my life. Please make sure that there is a mutual physical attraction and that this is a person who is reliable, trustworthy, available, and loves animals and kids. Please allow us to love each other fully and to be willing to grow together. Thank you from the bottom of my heart.

Pray from the Heart

It is a basic law of the Universe that what we put out is what we get back. The quantity and quality of the prayer energy we emit factors heavily into the result. When we pray from our heads, we say the words, but they carry little or no vigor with them. When we pray from our hearts, we call upon God with passion, purpose, and forcefulness. The increased energetic vibration creates resolution more quickly and efficiently. It also produces the amount of power necessary to open the gate to the Divine Mind during periods of time when our subconscious mind (or ego) is exerting control.

When praying from the heart, focus is given to each word concerning its substance and meaning. We are thinking about what we are saying as we articulate our appeal, and are infusing it with great importance.

Example:
(Weak) Oh Divine Master, I ask for peace and harmony within, that I may be of greater service. Thank you.

(Powerful) Oh Divine Master, I ask for peace and harmony within, that I may be of greater service! Thank you so much for showing me the way!

Include Gratitude

Gratitude is an important part of being prayerful. Remember that what we give out to the Universe circulates back to us. In other words, energetic vibrations of a certain nature attract like vibrations. When we focus on what we are grateful for, we increase the occurrence of circumstances for which we can be grateful. Gratitude puts our minds in a positive, appreciative, and hopeful place, which is in complete alignment with universal desire. It is, after all, God's wish that we be happy and fulfilled, for the God-Force is always attempting to create this. Therefore, gratitude tells the Universe that it is on the right track, and this again opens the gate to love, wisdom, and compassion.

Example:
God/Goddess, thank you so much for all you've given me—my family and my home, children to love and care for, and my wonderful dog! Today I ask for enough money to pay our bills each month and the strength to refrain from overspending. I ask this, for I know that if I could be peaceful about our finances, I would be calmer and kinder around my husband/wife/partner and children. Thank you so much for hearing my prayer and bringing me whatever I need to make this happen.

MEDITATION/CONTEMPLATION

Meditation is a quieting of the mind. It is a retreat of sorts, which moves us away from our outer, material world into the inner sanctuary of the higher mind. Just as we might take a bath or shower to rinse off physical dirt and toxins, meditation gives the mind a bath in a sea of compassion, serenity, and tenderness. It is a process through which ego material, such as worry, fear, or anger, can be managed, destabilized, and released into a sea of love and forgiveness. Contemplation goes hand in hand with different types of meditation. Therefore, I include the term here, although any contemplation that is categorically the same as meditation, is totally nonjudgmental, as is the practice of meditation. Meditation and contemplation help us to tune into Infinite Intelligence, thus, causing the gate between the conscious and superconscious minds to open and remain open for some time afterward.

I once went to an Ayurvedic doctor for a consultation on my health, to see what she might be able to offer me. After handing me a ten-page repertoire of Ayurvedic methods and remedies, and touching upon a few of these, she said to me, "If you do nothing else, at least meditate. That's the most important item on the list." Needless to say, I learned how to meditate and have kept up the practice for many years.

In the beginning, after taking my first class in transcendental meditation, I thought, "This is what meditation is." I wasn't wrong, but I found out later, through study and experience, that there were many different kinds of meditation, every one of them having merit. After a while, I began to choose the type that seemed appropriate for the moment, knowing there was no right or wrong way to practice. There was only what *felt* achievable to me at the time. This was because I had struggled with attention-deficit disorder (ADD) since I was young, and my concentration wasn't always top rate. Meditation was something I had to work at. Yet, it was always worth the effort, mainly because of the inner peace it produced. One advantage of having ADD and wanting to meditate, was that my condition forced me to research the meditation field in order to discover what would work best for me.

I found that sometimes I could quiet my mind, but at other times, all I could hear was chatter, chatter, chatter. Thus, I opted to use different kinds of meditation, depending on my state of mind that particular day. As I progressed in my understanding of meditation techniques, I was able to help clients and students key into their own personalized choices.

If you are a beginner at meditation, it might be advantageous to try one meditation technique for awhile, until you familiarize yourself with its methodology and effects. Then try another. Some of you may instantly know what would work for you and what might not. If that is the case, jump in wherever you're comfortable. If you are a more advanced meditator, you may still want to experiment with other methods if you have not already. Follow your instinct.

Below are listed some useful guidelines to follow during meditation. These are not hard and fast rules but simply guidelines to point us in a helpful direction. As always, experiment with what works best for you.

1. Wear comfortable clothing.

2. Keep your back as straight as possible, whether lying down or sitting.

3. Plan to meditate in a quiet environment. Unplug your telephone or go into a room that has no phone.

4. Explain to family members beforehand that you are going to meditate and that you would like to be left undisturbed during that time. With small children, use naptime for your meditation or contemplation, if possible. With older kids, put a sign up on your door whenever you want to meditate, assuming you have already offered them an explanation.

5. Make a commitment to meditate for a period of time each day or week. A good rule of thumb is fifteen to thirty minutes in the morning and fifteen to thirty minutes in the late afternoon or early evening. However, once a day or twice a day for less time can also be beneficial. If you can't meditate every day due to time constraints, try to pledge yourself to three to four times weekly for perhaps thirty minutes to one hour each time.

Now that the foundation has been laid, let's move on to different types of meditation/contemplation. In many forms of meditation, notice that the mind will always move to the places it needs to heal. Therefore, you may find yourself thinking about worrisome, fearful, or otherwise emotionally charged subject matter. Our goal is to allow these thoughts to be present without judging their existence. We merely notice them and gently bring our minds back to a neutral center point. In guided meditation or contemplative meditations, it is enough to consciously choose compassion when emotionally charged material arises. In a quiet, meditative state, this is usually easier to accomplish.

What follows are several types of meditation from which to choose. Space here is limited to simple explanations. For further study, see the bibliography at the end of this book or obtain meditation training from a meditation instructor.

1. Breathing: Sit quietly and focus on your breath. You may breathe long, deep breaths or breathe naturally. If you would like, you may say silently to yourself, "Breathing in …" on the inhale, and "Breathing out …" on the exhale. Anytime a thought arises, simply notice, and bring your attention back to the breath.

2. Mantra: Sit quietly and breathe deeply into your belly and up through your chest. On the out-breath, focus on one of the following tones (mantras), either silently or aloud: OHM …, AH …, RA …, EEM …, SHA … LOM …, P. E . A . C. E … You may also pick any other sound that you feel comfortable with. Again, if thoughts arise, merely notice them and gently bring your concentration back to your mantra.

3. Flame: Sit quietly with a candle in front of you. Focus your eyes on the flame. Keep your attention on the flickering light. Allow any negative thoughts and energy to flow out and to the light. You may visualize this when you have emotionally charged material that arises. As always, continue to bring your attention back to the flame over and over again.

4. Walking: Put on comfortable shoes and clothing. Breathe deeply into your belly and let nature in all her magnificent glory be what you focus your mind on. This gives your mind something to do and allows you to be in the present moment. If you can, pick one spot

in the sky or the trees on which to focus, until you must shift that focus to a new spot. Let any negative thought energy be released into nature to be neutralized and dissolved.

5. Cooking: Allow your mind to be focused on preparing your meal. Concentrate on every part of the preparation, from washing to peeling, chopping to cooking, smelling to tasting. Whenever other thoughts pop into your mind, notice them without judgment, and gently return to your cooking experience. This meditation can be done with any activity. It is known more formally as a type of mindfulness meditation.

6. Insight: The purpose of insight meditation is to gain understanding or acceptance of painful, pleasant, or neutral emotional states. It is also known as Vipassana Meditation in Buddhist philosophy, and is a form of mindfulness meditation.

   To begin, focus on the breath. As thoughts arise, pay attention to these thoughts and the feelings associated with them. See if you can let your feelings be, without resisting them, judging yourself for having them, or becoming attached to (lost in) them. You may want to examine your feelings, asking yourself where they stem from and what the thoughts are that are causing them. You may want to explore other choices that you have or what the physical sensations are that accompany your feelings. If you find that the feelings are unbearable, return your focus to your breath.

   Phrases that promote a nonjudgmental and accepting stance are:

   1. *"Oh well, if it happens, it happens,"*
   2. *"This is just old conditioning."*
   3. *"I surrender this to God."*

4. *"So, it's there, just let it be."*
5. *"I see you (thoughts), but I do not choose you."*

If those don't work, experiment, and find your own phrase that brings you to a place of acceptance. When caught up in an emotion or negative thought, use one of these phrases and return your attention to your breath.

7. Guided: Guided meditations are done by either listening to another person read to you, by listening to a tape or CD, or by reading to yourself, in which case, you can pause after each paragraph to fully visualize and experience the meaning of the words. Oftentimes, guided meditations take us on a journey for the purpose of calming our minds and embracing our inner reality. Guided meditations can be found at the end of many chapters in this book and in many tapes and books on the market.

Sample Guided Meditation

(A good one to use at the beginning of any meditation period.)

Grounding

Close your eyes and make yourself comfortable. Focus on your breathing ... breathing into your belly and up through your chest. Imagine breathing in calming energy, however you imagine that to be. Exhale all your tensions, conflict, and stress.

Now imagine that you have roots, roots like a tree, roots that branch out through all of the earth, through all the layers of the earth, pulling the earth's sustenance into your body ... nourishing earth energy ... pulling it up into your body as you inhale ... up through the soles of your feet ... flowing through all parts of your body ... and up into your head.

You might see this energy as a golden light, feeding all parts of you with its warmth and its beauty. Feel the supportive, nurturing, sustaining energy of this golden earth light surging through every cell of your body ... relaxing you ... enabling you to focus ... supplying you with strength and power ...

Now, visualize the top of your head opening up like a funnel, and Divine white light pouring in ... pouring into the whole of your body and tingling down your spine ... mixing harmoniously with the golden light energy of the earth. Both streams of light are entering your body simultaneously, and you feel at one with the earth and with the vast brightness of the Divine ... Relax into what this feels like ... and stay there until you feel thoroughly connected ... in harmony ... balanced ... at peace.

Now, as you open your eyes, know that as you focus your attention elsewhere, this energy will continue to sustain you and move through you, ground you, and center you ... for you are the earth, and you are Spirit ... and all is well.

AFFIRMATIONS

Affirmations are positive statements that contradict negative thoughts and thought groups that seem to control our minds. Through their use, we consciously choose to change our reality and create improved conditions in our lives. Affirmations operate through the universal law that states:

> Like creates like. We draw like a magnet to us those energetic frequencies that we give out. If we give out negative vibes, we will

attract negative people and/or circumstances to us and vice versa; if we give out positive vibes, we will attract positive people and/or circumstances.

When we think positively, the power of the superconscious mind is free to flow toward the conscious mind and therefore has an opportunity to express itself. Again, this is because positive thinking is in alignment with the goals of the Universe, that is, creating happiness and peace of mind. Filling our minds with higher, positive thought energies opens our gate. Negative thoughts close it.

Affirmations are stated in the present tense as though what we want is already happening. That is because if an affirmation is phrased in the future tense, improved conditions will always be waiting in the wings, so to speak—until such time as the Universe is clear that the conditions are wanted *now*! Wording our statement in the present tense doesn't mean that one's life improves immediately but that improvement has been set in motion and the specifics of what is desired are free to manifest in the now. There may be much that needs to change in order to manifest our desire, but now creation knows exactly where it is going.

Example:
Negative thought: I am so fat and ugly that I will never get a date.
Sample Affirmation: I am beautiful just the way I am and many men (women) are excited to go out with me.
Sample Affirmation: I am the perfect weight for me and I look lovely just the way I am. The right man (woman) for me is now at my side loving me totally.

As you can see, affirmations can be worded in different ways, depending upon what fits for each person. The main point is to word it in the present tense.

As with prayer, the more energy we put into affirmations and the more often we say them, the quicker and more thoroughly we receive what we are trying to create. Don't worry if it feels awkward to say an affirmation or if you don't believe it. It isn't expected that you believe it. This is the reason for articulating the positive thought in the first place. All you have to do is *pretend* you believe it. The mind will project outward whatever you feed it and, through time, as you can see circumstances change, your belief will automatically shift. Remember, change is a process and there may be many steps involved.

Since affirmations are used to create a new condition, the Universe may bring up blocks to its manifestation. This means that there may be some conditions that need to heal before the creation can show itself. Uncomfortable feelings might arise causing us to imagine that our affirmation is not working. This is not necessarily so. We are merely "in process." At other times when we use affirmations, we may feel better almost instantly. If we allow ourselves to merely perform the practice without expectations, we will move through the process quite easily.

We may have hundreds of negative thoughts per day and many of them are unconscious. We can't possibly handle all of them at once. Therefore, it is beneficial to choose one or two with which to work for a given time period. A time period of thirty days is a healthy place to start, although longer time periods may be needed and shorter time periods may produce great success.

Once we write down the appropriate affirmations, I suggest that you say them (passionately and from the heart) ten times in a row, three times daily. In addition, it is often helpful to write the affirmations ten times a day and to say them aloud. This adds additional power to the words.

During the time period we are practicing affirmations, it is advantageous to be as vigilant and conscious as possible. This is because negative thought patterns are like bad habits, hard to break.

If we are practicing our positive thinking but allowing our negative thought habits to run rampant, we may be canceling out our good work. Therefore, when we become aware that we are thinking in a destructive way, we can say to ourselves, "Cancel, Cancel," and immediately substitute our affirmation. The more often we can do this, the more effective our practice.

Below are listed some general affirmations you may find helpful. If you would like, you can reword them to suit your needs, after choosing one or two to which you feel drawn. You may also put two to three together in a short affirmative paragraph. If you are so inclined, work on this for thirty days and see what happens:

1. *I am confident and prosperous each day, knowing the God-Force is working through me and directing me.*

2. *If, during the day I don't feel well, I am positive that the healing power of the Divine within me will quickly restore me.*

3. *All conflict within me is gone, and I am completely peaceful today, knowing my higher self is guiding my every step.*

4. *The power of the Divine within me is greater than any obstacle facing me.*

5. *I glow with vibrations of prosperity and well-being wherever I may be each day.*

6. *My body is in perfect balance. All energy flows freely through me. My physical health is excellent!*

7. *I am in loving God-Consciousness twenty-four hours a day!*

8. *I am physically, emotionally, and spiritually healthy today, and I am filled with loving thoughts toward all.*

9. *I accept and love myself unconditionally, for I know I am a Divine being in physical form doing the best I can with what I presently know.*

The following is an affirmative prayer of protection from the Unity philosophy:

The Light of God surrounds me.
The Love of God enfolds me.
The Power of God protects me.
The Presence of God watches over me.
Wherever I am, God is, and ALL is well.

PRESENT MOMENTING

When our subconscious mind is ruling our lives, we generally find ourselves reacting to life situations from a place of fear, anger, or any gamut of negative emotions. We are on autopilot, and often have no conscious awareness of why we're feeling the way we do. Even if we understand the source of our emotions, we may feel as though we have little or no control over them. In addition to all the tools we've discussed so far, present momenting offers us another way to manage "ego material" and operate from our hearts with love and wisdom.

Because the subconscious mind is a memory bank of emotionally charged data, its substance arises from past experiences. As has been stated, this energy flows constantly toward the conscious mind to be expressed out into the world. As we interact with others, old emotional issues get triggered again and again if we do not work to resolve them. Each moment of life can become an instant in which old hurts and wounds are reactivated in the present moment.

In addition, when we are on autopilot, we are not aware of our choices and we tend to project our past into our future, believing that our future will contain the exact contents of our past. That is what happens when someone who has gone through a devastating divorce moves into a new relationship, and worries that this union, too, will break up in the future. Someone who has been taught that being skinny will bring praise and being plump will produce scorn, may feel guilty and anxious when she eats even a bite of fattening food. Thus, all fear and guilt springs from the past and often becomes worry about the future.

As we go about our days, we often find ourselves living in the past or in the future. That is, we react to instead of acting upon life circumstances and therefore, create a stressful reliving of old experiences and worry about new occurrences. In contrast, when we consciously choose to bring our attention into the present moment, we loosen the grip of our destructive emotional thought. This is because fear and worry exist only in the past and the future. Sensation or feeling that resides in the present moment is manageable without the addition of fear, worry, guilt, and regret, which are past and future emotions.

For example, if we imagine a disturbing situation in which our boss is condemning us for something we did and disparaging our character, we may feel our muscles tensing, our body heating up, our face turning red, our heart beating fast, or the like. We may also remember our anger or apprehension when our parents used to continually criticize us. But if we are focused in the present moment, we can recognize these as simple sensations or feelings that will ultimately pass, without worrying about whether we will be fired, how we will pay our bills, or if someone else will ever hire such a deficient employee. When we dwell on the past or the future, we become lost in the emotionally charged memories and imaginings we feed ourselves. It is only in the present moment that Divine love and wisdom can effectively reach our conscious mind and imbue it with the ability to choose compassion for ourselves and our boss. With the help of Infinite Intelligence, we can choose to accept our sensations as a human response to a difficult situation. We can choose to see our boss as someone who has his own problems, his own fears. Even though our past might be triggered in the now, we need not perpetuate its existence into our future or intensify an already emotional situation.

This truth is articulated beautifully in an e-mail which I received long ago. The author is unknown:

Think This Over

There are two days of every week about which we should not worry, two days which should be kept free from fear and apprehension.

One of these days is yesterday with its mistakes and cares, its faults and blunders, its aches and pains. Yesterday has passed forever beyond our control.

All the money in the world cannot bring back yesterday. We cannot undo a single act we performed; we cannot erase a single word we said. Yesterday is gone.

The other day we should not worry about is tomorrow, with its possible adversaries, its burdens, its large promise and poor performance. Tomorrow is also beyond our immediate control.

Tomorrow's sun will rise, whether in splendor or behind a mask of clouds—but it will rise. Until it does, we have no stake in tomorrow, for it is as yet unborn.

That leaves only one day—today. Any man can fight the battles of just one day. It is only when you and I add the burdens of these two awful eternities—yesterday and tomorrow—that we break down.

It is not the experience of today that drives men mad, it is remorse or bitterness for something that happened yesterday and the dread of what tomorrow may bring.

Let us, therefore, live but one day at a time.

Thus, the idea is to consciously work on redirecting our attention back to the present moment. In a way, it is a form of meditation in which the present moment is our center point. Whenever we find ourselves in a situation we're not confident we can handle, we are feeling overwhelmed. Often this occurs because our minds have moved backward or forward in time. The center point of the present moment stabilizes our emotional system, allowing greater clarity, creativity, and compassion to flow from the God-Mind, and offering greater opportunity for resolution of whatever challenge we're facing.

Acceptance

Acceptance is such an important tool that I've devoted the whole next chapter to the concept. However, it's worth mentioning here with the other tools of the trade because of its significance in opening the gate to the superconscious mind and allowing the Universe to work on our behalf. When we resist circumstances that come into our lives, it is as though we are waging war against Infinite Intelligence and our battle is because we think we know better than the God-Force what we need or want. Internally, we are saying to our life situation, "Stay away," in an attempt to stem the flow of what appears to be monstrous and unbearable but is really goodness in disguise. It takes enormous energy to resist and the results are often burnout, fatigue, rage, depression, or anxiety. As you can imagine, fighting a force the size of the Universe is quite overwhelming and always unsuccessful, to some degree.

When we accept what life hands us, we are trusting God to run our lives, and therefore, unbolting the Divine gate that closes off during resistance. In the very act of acceptance, we allow the God-Force to give us everything it's got, including the ability to handle anything that comes along. When we resist, we are on our own, without all the resources and support that Universal Intelligence is willing and able to offer. During resistance we struggle, we cry, we kick, we scream, either figuratively or actually. Acceptance guarantees that we will walk through the briars and brambles more calmly, more empowered, and more successfully, attaining wisdom along the way.

This poem by Rumi describes acceptance in a profound and exquisite way.

The Guest House

This being human is a guest house.
Every morning is a new arrival.
A joy, a depression, a meanness,
some momentary awareness comes
as an unexpected visitor.

Welcome and entertain them all!
Even if they're a crowd of sorrows,
who violently sweep your house
empty of its furniture,
still, treat each guest honorably.
He may be clearing you out
for some new delight.

The dark thought, the shame, the malice,
meet them at the door laughing,
and invite them in.

Be grateful for whoever comes,
because each has been sent
as a guide from beyond.

EFFECTIVE EXPRESSION OF FEELINGS

Long ago Jerry Jampolsky, MD, the father of the International Attitudinal Healing movement, wrote his first book, *Love Is Letting Go of Fear.* In his book, Dr. Jampolsky stressed the importance of releasing fear and other negative emotions in order to open our hearts fully to love. He further asserted that being in a state of love was the key to living a life of inner peace. Jerry, as many of us know him, spent his lifetime helping people all over the world create sacred, safe groups in which to do this very work of expressing and releasing difficult feelings. He believed, as I do, that once this was accomplished, people could join together in unity, harmony, and peace, just the way Divine Creation intended. In the many years that I've been fortunate to be a part of the Detroit, Michigan, Attitudinal Healing Center, I have seen countless persons transformed through education and emotional release, introducing them to states of peace and love that they had never before experienced.

As living beings, we were designed to evolve and we were given the necessary apparatus to move debris out of the way so that we could advance forward in our growth. Just as physical toxins are moved out of our bodies via our bowels, our nasal passages and our skin, etc., psychic toxins are discharged through crying, talking, screaming, shaking, and the like. We all know that if a discharge system of the physical body is clogged, the resulting condition can make us quite ill. The same is true for the emotional system of the body.

When feelings are repressed for any length of time, they can wreak havoc within the psychological as well as the physical state of our being. This is why cancer patients are often urged to work on resolving psychological issues which have plagued them for a long time.

As our soul progresses through the evolutionary process, it undergoes, through different personalities and over many lifetimes, many emotionally laden experiences. The soul's suffering is recorded in its memory bank, which takes the form of the subconscious mind in physical form. Memories are stored as energy throughout the cells of the body, for every cell possesses memory. As emotions are retriggered in life situations, they are either healed and dissolved through effective expression, or they are weighted down with additional emotional charge and returned to the subconscious. When emotional conditions are not resolved over long periods of time, the associated energy becomes stuck inside the body, causing disease, physically and/or mentally.

With this in mind, we can see that effective expression of feelings is a most significant part of the soul's drive toward happiness and peace. What is effective expression? We might say, for instance, "I cried and cried, but to no avail." Effective expression of feelings requires that love, nonjudgment, compassion, and understanding be present during the time of emotional release. This is because negativity cannot exist in the presence of love. In time, it loses its power, melting and disappearing into its positive counterpart. If love could be likened to water in the *Wizard of Oz,* it would dissolve fear and other emotional pain, just as water destroyed the Wicked Witch of the West.

Ineffective expression of feelings might occur when we're fighting with our spouse, screaming at each other because we think we're right and they're wrong. They may be screaming back, having felt attacked. Nowhere in this scenario is there a compassionate listener, and no way is this going to resolve in such a manner. In this case, our anger is recharged, weighted down with heavier emotion, and returned to our subconscious mind to be retriggered at a later date. This demonstrates that all expression of feeling is not equal. That is why many of us become frustrated when we think we are releasing emotions but it's not working to bring about the peace we desire. There is simply more to it than crying, screaming, or talking. Love, in some fashion, must be present.

Consequently, it's important to seek out someone who can offer nonjudgment, compassionate listening and understanding. This can be provided by a teacher, a therapist, a minister or rabbi, a support group member, a friend, a family member, or one's higher self. If you are by yourself when discharging emotion, be particularly mindful of your thoughts as you go through the process. If you are belittling yourself in any way for having these feelings, you will be less effective in resolving them. Go easy on yourself. Allow yourself to see the humanness in you, and understand that you must release these emotions in order to see more clearly, to open your heart to greater love, and to find the inner peace you long for.

Please remember that the process of evolution is a continuous one. Sometimes we have layer upon layer of emotional charge built up. We may release one layer, but still have more to go. We must be patient with ourselves and remember that we are making progress every time we release feelings in the presence of loving kindness. Often it is helpful to visualize the process as if we were emptying out a giant glass of spoiled milk and refilling it with sweet cream. The spoiled milk represents the negative emotion that has built up and the cream represents new knowledge, wisdom—a way of perceiving everyone and everything in the world through the eyes of love. As we spill out some of the spoiled milk, we can pour in an equal amount of cream. We go back and forth until the giant glass is filled only with cream. This, of course, may take lifetimes, but with effort, a great deal can be accomplished right now. *Effective emotional expression* is essential to the opening of our gate. Through its use, our thought and activity become increasingly enveloped in the goodness of the Divine.

SEEKING SUPPORT

At the beginning of my spiritual journey, I hibernated for months, letting go of negative emotions and avidly reading all the metaphysical material I could find, because I was drawn to learning new ways of relating to my world. The ideas I considered during my reading sessions were wonderfully enlightening, but I longed for people with whom to share thoughts, stories, and common experiences. Often, I was lonely and yearned to be understood and heard. The only support I had had was from those who still operated from fear-based thinking, and I needed to be surrounded by people centered on love, growth, and spirituality. I prayed about this extensively and eventually found myself at an initial workshop that looked interesting, and which led to a *Course in Miracles* class and an attitudinal healing conference, where I felt like I had come home. So began my journey into the world of people again—only this time, I had found like-minded individuals who supported my growth into new directions, and it felt like an enormous breath of fresh air.

When we embark on our voyage toward internal transformation, we must often leave behind old, obsolete support systems that pull us back into destructive thinking and activity patterns. That doesn't mean that we must stop seeing familiar friends and family members, but we might choose to spend less time with them or refrain from talking to them about our problems, interests, or desires. When we are being introduced to brand-new ideas and information, we are like baby trees that are planted but need stakes to sustain their growth. As our knowledge expands and we settle into our new self, our need for support diminishes but never disappears completely. Even larger trees require sunshine, rain, and appropriate soil for nourishment and preservation. We've all heard the expression, "No man is an island." This is especially true when attempting to navigate the journey toward peace. It's tough for a sailor to steer his ship through a storm. The way is found more easily with the help of a group of qualified buddies. Seeking peace can be a turbulent journey occasionally, and our will may collapse from time to time. Being surrounded by others who understand our pain, our frustrations, and our joys can be the very buoy we need to keep afloat during such times.

Loving support also offers us the environment in which inner transformation most easily occurs and constructive attitudes and perceptions emerge. Remember that negativity cannot exist for long in the presence of love and compassion. Sometimes all that is needed is a caring and wise friend who will allow us to talk through our troubles, empathize with our feelings, and set us on the path toward forgiveness. For many years I had a special friend (who recently passed away) who was my go-to person whenever I was particularly distressed about something. I performed the same role for her. The beauty of the situation was that we were on similar paths of personal growth and could both listen lovingly to each other complain or cry and help one another realign our thinking. When she was going through a difficult divorce, my nonjudgmental attentiveness allowed her to scream out her anger and yet return eventually to a place of forgiveness and understanding. When I suffered through the illness and death of my father, her compassion allowed me to grieve appropriately without becoming totally lost in my sadness. She helped me to see death through new eyes and to grow past my old limitations.

If we liken ourselves to a community of geese, we can understand the importance of support. A student of mine gave me the following article:

The Sense of a Goose

This spring, when you see geese returning north for the summer, flying along in a "V" formation ... you might consider what science has discovered as to why they fly that way. As each bird flaps its wings, it creates an uplift for the bird immediately following. By flying in a "V" formation, the whole flock adds at least 71 percent greater flying range than if each bird flew on its own.

People who share a common direction and sense of community can get where they are going more quickly and easily because they are traveling on the thrust of one another. When a goose falls out of formation, it suddenly feels the drag and resistance of trying to go it alone … and quickly gets back into formation to take advantage of the lifting power of the bird in front … and geese honk from behind to encourage those up front to keep up the speed.

Finally, and this is important, when a goose gets sick, or is wounded by gunshots and falls out of formation, two other geese fall out with the goose and follow it down to lend help and protection. They stay with the fallen goose until it is able to fly or until it dies, and only then do they launch out on their own, or with another formation to catch up with their group.
If we have as much sense as a goose, we will stay in formation with those who are headed in the same direction we are …

If we have the sense of a goose, we will stand by each other like they do.

—Dr. Harry Clarke Noyes

GRATITUDE

In the course of a lifetime, we may confront many hurdles, obstacles, problems, and frustrations as well as a multitude of delights and pleasures. Life is certainly unpredictable and can be tough or joyous. It is easy to focus on the positive in happy times, but during times of stress and strain, it's often easier to see the glass half empty. Luckily, we have been provided with a mind capable of choice, and if we look hard enough during trying times, there are always blessings of which to be aware.

Bringing our attention to that for which we're thankful opens the gate to the superconscious mind, bringing a rush of goodness into one's experience and conscious awareness. Using gratitude is a way of aligning the mind with God consciousness, for the God-Mind consists only of constructive and optimistic energy. Appreciative thoughts increase all good in our lives because of the universal law that states, *Whatever we think about expands,* or, in other words, what we put out is what we get back.

If we are thinking about what we don't have, we may perpetuate the lack of that very thing in our lives. Conversely, if our minds are thankful for what we *do have,* we will surely bring more into our lives for which to be grateful. If it is financial security we're looking for, we might focus on all the money we have at the present time and be thankful for the ability to pay whatever bills we are able. We can even be appreciative for the change in our pockets. If it is love or friendship we want more of, we can look for any love or support there might already be in our life and be grateful for that.

Think about people in your life who always thank you and appreciate you when you give to them. Do you not feel like giving more to them? The Universe has the same nature. When we offer our thanks for what we've been given, the Universe enjoys our appreciation and is quick to bring us more of what has created its enjoyment. Our Divine Source wants to please us, for giving is its natural state.

People who are appreciative receive the abundance this good earth has to offer. They have opened their hearts to receiving it through their very attitude of gratefulness. Thankfulness carries with it contentment and fulfillment. We feel safe and peaceful when we are in a grateful state of mind. Therefore, we become an open receptacle upon whom the Universe may shower its bounty

There are many ways to practice gratitude. Below are some specific ideas:

1. Take ten minutes each night to review the events of your day, looking for anything for which to be grateful. Express your thanks to God.

2. Make a list of people, things, or circumstances for which you're

grateful. This can include family, friends, gifts, jobs, rest, trips, accomplishments, talents, skills, weather, etc. All aspects of life can be examined here. Either make new weekly lists or focus on one general list once or twice a day. You can also make an ongoing list.

3. If you have a difficult time finding things for which to be...grateful, explore how you might identify some of these. You can be grateful for the smallest items: a place to sleep, a roof over your head, food to eat, clothes to wear, completion of a minor job or chore, a sunrise or sunset, etc.

4. Look for ways to acknowledge and demonstrate your gratitude. Thank-you notes, e-mails, visits, gifts, help with tasks, or giving attention to someone are ideas to get you started.

5. Be grateful for your life. You are truly blessed to be on this earth learning and growing at all times! *The Tibetan Book of Living and Dying* by Sogyal Rinpoche says that many souls clamor to be born into bodies, but that a limited number are accepted into this earthly existence at one time. Living in this existence is truly a fortunate circumstance because of the opportunities available here for the evolvement of the soul.

LEARNING THROUGH EXPERIENCE

1. *Consider the tools you've just explored. How many of them have you utilized in your life and for how long? Which ones are easier for you to use than others? What would you like to try that you haven't?*

2. *Pick one or more of the following:*

    a. *Choose two to three tools to practice for one month. Record your results in a journal.*
    b. *Make a contract with yourself to practice using one tool each week for nine weeks. Note your experience with each one.*
    c. *Explore the areas of meditation and prayer. Compare your experiences. You may write your findings in a journal, if you wish.*
    d. *Think of three times in the recent past that you have felt troubled or conflicted. Identify which tools you might have used at the time to help you find inner peace.*
    e. *Write down all "Tools of the Trade" on a sheet of paper or a 3x5 card. Copy the list several times and put one in each room of your house, in your car, and at work. Refer to this list whenever you feel any negative emotion.*

Surrender is an act of humility,
an acknowledgment that life is a
mystery whose depth the mind
cannot fathom.

—Dan Millman

CHAPTER 9

The Art of True Surrender

MY first true experience of surrender occurred on a beautiful summer day in 1991. Although I had studied the concept of surrender, my comprehension was still limited to what I could rationally understand in my head, leaving my heart untouched by such profound knowledge.

It all began in May, when I noticed sensations of cramps and pain in my abdomen. Originally, I made light of it, assuring myself that it would disappear, that I was just having my usual mild stomach irritation. But as time progressed, I began to think that something was very wrong. The pain was increasing, and I knew I had better see a doctor, which I proceeded to do after about four weeks. The doctor, an MD versed in naturopathic medicine, first began to prescribe natural remedies for me, all of which I tried but to no avail. Next came the tests, during which I spent hours in uncomfortable preparation and then more time in the hospital for procedures. A month later

I learned that the tests had revealed nothing easily treatable and that the label "irritable/inflammatory bowel syndrome" had been placed on my record.

Further steps included working with a holistic clinic that offered homeopathic remedies. That was very encouraging, and I do believe the remedies were helpful, but I found very quickly that for me, the process of working with homeopathy could be challenging. It was hard work for me, and the pain intensified as I began to toil through emotional issues on a psycho-spiritual level.

During this time period of approximately three months, I began to feel extremely depressed, as I realized that my physical problems might not be temporary. I might have to deal with such symptoms on and off during the course of my life. I felt withdrawn and unmotivated. I would do only what I had to do and no more. I would go to populated places, but I felt alone and different. I wept every day as I struggled to deal with severe intestinal pain, and although I tried, I had great difficulty removing my focus from the pain. And so, during those months, I prayed to God to take this pain away–far, far away. And I prayed constantly, believing that if I prayed hard enough the God-Force would surely answer me and appease my desire.

By August, I was feeling exhausted—mentally, physically, and emotionally, but from the depths of my soul, there still was the unending drive to transcend my circumstances, to learn all I could from them and to triumph in spite of it all. And so, as usually happens in the course of intense growth and transformation, one memorable morning, I finally learned the lesson the Universe had been trying to teach me. The impact was so strong, that I know I will never forget it.

I was taking my usual bike ride and crying my usual tears, asking God where he/she was, when I suddenly felt I could not go on. I felt the struggle so great that I stopped my bike on a private road, looked up into the heavens through the treetops and beseeched the Divine to show me what to do. I felt, as I looked up, that although I was standing physically, that my whole being lay helpless on the ground, limp and utterly fatigued without an ounce of strength left. And as I looked up, I heard for the first time how I had created darkness in my life and what I could do to bring in the light.

The voice inside my head said, "Accept the will and wisdom of God. As long as you try to push it away, the light cannot reach you." And what I realized in that exquisite moment was that ever since this all had begun, I had resisted its presence in my life. I hadn't trusted Infinite Intelligence to bring me my highest good. My loss of faith had brought darkness and despair, and my inability to accept the work that had been given me in this lifetime was killing my spirit and stealing all my energy.

As the dawning of this new awareness spread through my being, I found myself uttering words of acceptance to this Universal Force, and begging for the ability to endure this load. As the day progressed, I discovered, for the first time in three months, a newfound strength and perseverance and an extraordinary lifting of my mood. It was as though I were magically transformed. It felt no less than miraculous!

The light in me began to glow again that day, as I recognized that there really was nothing to fear. The realization was that complete surrender, which involved total acceptance of my circumstances, was the way through the dark and terrifying tunnel of fear. I knew then that meeting my dragons in this lifetime would never be quite the same again. I had discovered one of the great secrets of the Universe.

When I introduce the idea of surrender to students or clients, without fail, some of them will question the wisdom of such a practice. To many, it feels like giving up control, which can seem frightening, especially when dealing with already emotional situations. Ironically, however, the true act of surrender generates a kind of peaceful tranquility, a steady resolve, and often, tremendous joy as is apparent in the following two stories. Although I do not know the authors, these stories deeply touched my life and the lives of the individuals who gave them to me.

A woman had been ill for six months with a widespread lung infection, and persistent prayer had resulted in nothing. She was still in bed full time.

One afternoon, a pamphlet was placed in her hands that changed her life forever. In the pamphlet was the story of a missionary who had been an invalid for eight years. Constantly she had prayed that God would make her well so that she might do God's work. Finally, worn out with the futile petition, she prayed, "All right. I give up. If you want me to be an invalid, that's your business. Anyway, I want You even more than I want health. You decide." In two weeks the woman was out of bed, completely well.

This made no sense to the woman with the lung disease, and yet, she could not forget the story. And so, finally, with this story in her memory, one day she came to the same point of abject acceptance. She said to God, "I'm tired of asking. I'm beaten through, God. You decide what you want for me." Tears flowed. She describes in her own words what happened next.
"It was as if I had touched a button that opened windows in heaven; as if some dynamo of heavenly power began flowing, flowing. Within a few hours, I had experienced the presence of God in a way that wiped away all doubt and revolutionized my life. From that moment, my recovery began."

And another:

Mrs. Nathaniel Hawthorne, wife of the famous American author, had a similar experience, as she wrestled in prayer in the city of Rome one

February day in 1860. Una, the Hawthorne's eldest daughter, was dying of a virulent form of malaria. The attending physician, Dr. Franco, had, that afternoon, warned that unless the young girl's fever abated before morning, she would die.

As Mrs. Hawthorne sat by Una's bed, she thought to herself, "Una cannot die. She must not die! This daughter of ours has the finest mind and the most complex character of all our children. Why should some capricious Providence demand that we give her up?
As the night deepened, the girl lay so still that she seemed to be in the anteroom of death. The mother went to the window and looked out on the piazza. There was no moonlight; a dark and silent sky was heavy with clouds.

And she thought to herself, "I cannot bear this loss. I cannot—I cannot . . . " Then suddenly, unaccountably, another thought took over. "Why should I doubt the goodness of God? Let Him take Una, if He sees best. I can give her to him. No, I won't fight against Him anymore."

Then an even stranger thing happened. Having made the great sacrifice, Mrs. Hawthorne expected to feel sadder. Instead, she felt lighter, happier than at any time since Una's long illness had begun. Some minutes later, she walked back to the girl's bedside and felt her daughter's forehead. It was moist and cool. Una was sleeping naturally. And the mother rushed into the next room to tell her husband that a miracle had happened.

As we can see from these stories, the act of surrender can create powerful moments of enlightenment. When we finally let go of our control, universal energy is free to operate within us and for us. It is then that we become aware of our basic nature: peace and harmony. When we resist, we hurt. When we surrender, we fly. The God-Force is always looking to assist and encourage us. When we oppose its will, we block essential support from reaching us. It is for this reason that our acceptance of the will of God is so crucial.

ATTACHMENT

As human beings, we all look for pleasure and ease of living. Our unhealed mind (the lower self) often thinks it has all the answers to living peacefully. Its mind-set believes in the power of the external world to bring happiness and contentment. It doesn't yet realize that true happiness comes only from the inside. When the lower self is in charge, our mind becomes attached to (or stuck on) certain external outcomes.

In the stories above, attachment to health outcomes was a commonality. But other end results, to which we might attach, include:

- Being successful with a work project
- Earning a certain amount of money
- Getting our spouses or partners to see it our way
- Seeing our children or spouses give up drugs or alcohol
- Ridding ourselves of depression or anxiety
- Seeing our children get good grades/go to college/finish high school, etc.
- Losing a certain amount of weight/looking a particular way
- Obtaining a particular job
- Finding a soulmate

And the list goes on and on.

When we look at these often emotional desires, we can understand why it might be difficult to relinquish control and rely on a source that is invisible and sometimes questionable to us. Our belief systems, still immature, tell us that these are the very results we need in order to feel safe, secure, comfortable, and content. We cannot yet comprehend that it is only through Infinite Intelligence (our Divine Source) that we can assure our long-lasting protection and well-being. Consequently, it is helpful to review some basic ideas and their relationship to the art of surrender.

BASIC CONCEPTS

1. God (the Universe) is the energy of all good for all living things, and a power that is perfectly loving and all knowing in nature. In God's infinite intelligence we are created with everything we need to find our way to lasting peace and pleasure. It is as though the Divine has planted a seed inside of us, which is programmed to create only happiness and good. Just as an apple seed can produce only apple trees, we are programmed to produce only that which is beneficial, including kindness, decency, integrity, and lovingness. The art of surrender is recognizing that there's already that special something inside of us that knows how to bring peace, harmony, and joy. The Divine Mind would never let us suffer pointlessly because it already knows what we need to reach total contentment and joy.

2. There is a Universal will often unknown to our conscious will (self-will). The Universal will loves us and supports us more than our conscious will. Our self-will, *if unaligned with Universal will*, interferes with what we really want. It blocks us from our natural birthright of peace and joy. As human beings, God gives us free will and will not interfere with that free will. Therefore, we must let go

voluntarily of self-will in order for God to supply the energy and resources necessary for our natural growth toward good. That is why we feel highly supported when we accept God's will, and alone, angry or dejected when we resist.

3. What we thirst for is something beyond this world (inner peace). There's nothing in the world that can bring us the peace we're looking for. Healing is of the mind. Peace and happiness reside in the mind and in the way we perceive our existence. Moments of deep surrender are powerful catalysts for healing our erroneous perceptions of ourselves and our world.

4. Detachment from outcomes opens the gate for all good to flow toward us. Grasping closes it. The more we surrender, the more the physical world is set in motion to fortify us. The more we let go of self-will, the more good we attract to us.

5. We may not understand our circumstances or the choices God would have us make, but we will comprehend everything at a later time. Even if we do not understand it in this lifetime, eternity spreads before us, and there will come a time when all that we have learned is put to use for the betterment of others.

6. Surrender comes from the heart. We do not surrender intellectually or by "trying" to think it through. When we have had a true moment of surrender, we feel it and know it deeply. As in all transformational activity, learning the art of surrender is a process. Therefore, each step along the way is essential.

7. Fear is like a screen erected between us and God so that God's power cannot come through to us. Surrender is looking fear full in the face, instead of running away from it. It is remembering that

God's power is still the supreme reality and can only ultimately produce safety and security.

8. The Bible says, "Seek ye first the kingdom of heaven, and all else will be added unto you." To *surrender* is to be inspired, to be saved, to access miracles.

PRACTICING THE ART OF SURRENDER

As mentioned in number 6 above, the art of surrender is a process. Before I was able to let go of my self-will, I spent many years examining deep emotional issues and, more specifically, three long months spent in prayer and agony. Had I known what I know now, it might have been easier, but I didn't understand at the time what I needed to do to find my peaceful center. I was in process and every step along the way served to bring me to where I am today. Hopefully, my experience can now be helpful to others.

If you are working on mastering the art of surrender, you might try the following:

1. Find a quiet place where you can sit in silent awareness. Call upon your Higher Power (God, the Universe, Buddha, Jesus, Great Spirit, etc.) in prayer.

2. Listen to, or sense, your next step. If you don't hear or feel anything right away, continue to pray. Your prayer might be a simple request to be able to accept God's will and to be shown the way. You may need to repeat this step several times before you get a sense of what to do next.

3. When you feel a strong urge to do something, follow it. Examples of next steps might be to:

- Acknowledge and express your feelings.
- Discuss your feelings with a trusted friend, therapist or support group participant.
- Say, write, or think affirmations, such as,
    - "I am safe in the hands of God"
    - "I have 100 percent faith in the Universe"
    - "I surrender to the power of goodness and love"
    - "I am now ready to surrender."
- Take time to read a particular spiritual book or listen to a certain spiritual tape.
- Sign up for a class or lecture.

Follow your instinct and listen to your inner guidance for as long as it takes to let go of your own conscious will. As mentioned above, you may have to repeat these steps over and over before you actually master this concept. Learning to surrender can take time, persistence, and patience. However, sometimes it happens spontaneously.

Remember that your willingness to surrender is all that's necessary. You will understand the concept first in your head, and then in your heart. In the heart is where miracles occur.

LEARNING THROUGH EXPERIENCE

A. *Try the following exercise. You may want to write down your thoughts afterwards:*

- *What's one thing you're really afraid of?*
- *What outcome are you attached to?*
- *What blocks you from surrendering to the will of the Universe? What do you imagine will happen if you surrender your self-will?*
- *Think about what you're afraid of again, and notice how your body feels.*
  Do you notice rigidity or tenseness?
- *Now, lie on the floor, relaxed, as if you are a spaghetti noodle.*
- *Think about the love that the Universe has for you.*
- *Affirm your safety and protection. Imagine that you are placing your fear in a container of some sort and that God's loving light is surrounding it, transforming it, and removing it from your presence. Remember to relax and allow this process. Watch as your fear disappears from sight.*
- *Rise up empowered and repeat to yourself three times, "I am safe and peaceful no matter what is happening in my life."*

B. *Practice the following prayer each morning upon arising:*

SURRENDER PRAYER

Today, God, this is your day.
May I be who you would have me be,
May I do what you would have me do,
May I go where you would have me go,
Say what you would have me say,

and Dear Lord, as it is my deepest faith,
That as I so step back,
You shall step forward.
As I surrender, you shall take Divine authority.
I ask only that Your will be done in me and in all things.
Thank you, God.
AMEN

—Marianne Williamson

Intuition is the long-lost juice of life.
It brings us fluidity and joy, instantaneous answers,
and abundant knowledge just for the asking.
Living by intuition is an art that when mastered
produces a thrill like no other.

—Penney Peirce

Chapter 10

Intuition

I grew up with a highly developed intuitive sense and early on, attempted to live my life accordingly. But, as childhood advanced to adolescence, I found that my trust in inner guidance was fading away. My dear father was a logical fellow and extremely scientific in his approach to most things. Consequently, if I stated an opinion about something, I needed material proof to back up my assumptions in order to earn Dad's respect. If my reasoning could not be supported in a reputable book or magazine, it was not good enough.

Many of my teachers in school espoused a similar "scientific" viewpoint, which added greatly to this influence in my life. As time wore on, I began to doubt my deep inner knowingness about personal decisions, beliefs, and actions. To avoid rejection, I allowed my father and then others to dictate how I lived my life. I was never sure of my ideas, often asking others what I should do. The problem was, *their* answers weren't necessarily good for me.

As a matter of fact, most of the time, others had no idea what was good for me, even when they thought they did. As I grew older, through much internal struggle, I realized that I needed to take my power back and learn to trust my own instincts. After all, I was the one living my life—nobody else.

Slowly then, I began to come back to myself by listening increasingly to my own inner guidance, that sixth sense that helped with decisions and offered information that would direct me in solving life's challenges. Through time, I began to feel more alive, more fulfilled, and more confident, as I noticed that my dreams were beginning to come true and I was accomplishing things I never thought I could before. Most of all, I found myself less fearful as I came to understand that there was real power inside of me, the kind of power that could make lemonade out of lemons and that would fill me with awe and wonder time and again.

I now feel humbled and amazed by the power of intuition as I recall the many times in my life in which following my gut saved me, boosted me forward, or unraveled great mysteries for me. One of those times occurred when my seventy-three-year-old father was dying from lung cancer. I loved my dad deeply in spite of the fact that we didn't quite see eye to eye on certain subjects. We were emotionally quite similar and seemed to have a bond with one another, which went beyond this physical world.

During the summer that my dad was pronounced terminally ill, I had been back and forth many times between Detroit (where I live) and Cleveland (where I grew up and where my father still lived). However, my son was away at camp in Wisconsin and my husband and I had flown up to see him for a parent's weekend. I had stacks of work to do at home, so I wasn't planning to go back to Cleveland until Friday of the next week. When we arrived back in Detroit on Sunday, we unpacked and went to bed. I had been praying all week for my father's comfort and that he be surrounded by his loved ones as much as possible. I knew he had fear about the situation in which he found himself and deep guilt about causing his family such pain. I longed for him to be at peace and to reassure him to the best of my ability.

No one knew how long Dad had to live, but the doctors were stupefied by his condition. He had been diagnosed a mere three months earlier in May, had had surgery, and was expected to live quite a while longer. CAT scans had revealed no further cancer and his physicians were guardedly positive about full recovery. However, my father never recuperated enough even to come home. He remained hospitalized while doctors searched for answers. By the end of July, doctors felt they could do no more for him and pronounced him terminal. In spite of that, they felt he might hold on for months.

Lying in bed that Sunday night, I tossed and turned until I ultimately fell into a fitful sleep. In the middle of the night I awoke suddenly with the strongest urge to pack my bags again and go to Cleveland right then and there. By this time, I had practiced following my intuition for several years and knew its power. I *had* to pay attention. And so, after explaining this to my husband and attempting to rest until daylight, I arose early, grabbed a few clothes and toiletries, and set out on the road once more. When I arrived at the hospital, my father was sitting up and was more lucid than he had been in some time. He hadn't been eating much, but with help, he actually got out of bed, sat in a chair, and ate a whole bowl of frozen yogurt. I was able to spend the day with him, and although I left that night exhausted, I was overjoyed that I'd been able to be there with him.

At 5:00 a.m. the next morning, the phone rang, and my dad's nurse reported that he had passed away peacefully a few minutes before. At first I was stunned, as we were not expecting this to happen so soon, but when I reviewed the events of the previous two days, I realized that the God-Force was deeply at work within me for the benefit of my father and, as it turned out, for the rest of my family as well. The power of intuition—Divine Spirit's voice—had spoken once again, and by heeding its call, everything worked out in the best way possible. Ironically, the very man who opposed the use of intuition was greatly comforted because of it. Perhaps he and I both furthered our learning that day.

WHAT IS INTUITION?

As we have stated before, each of us is connected to Infinite Intelligence—that Divine wisdom that works only for our highest good. As is characteristic of anything spiritual, we may not be able to see or measure intuition, but rather, we feel it deep inside of us. It is the inaudible voice of Spirit, which speaks through revelations, insights, and strong urges. It is our messenger from a higher plane, a link to Divine wisdom or knowledge.

Sometimes it is helpful to understand what intuition *is* by noting what it's *not*. Intuition is *not* the mind that works vigorously to figure everything out. It does *not* work like a calculator that goes A + B + C = D. It does *not* weigh all the evidence—the pros and cons—in the attempt to draw conclusions about what to do in a particular situation. Using intuition is simply *not* a logical process. This doesn't mean that intuitive wisdom asks you to disregard rationality, judiciousness, or reason. To the contrary, intuition may ask you to use all of these tools on your journey. However, these means are secondary to our use of inner gut feelings. By using intuition, we can connect instantly with all the answers we puzzled about for months or attempted to solve logically.

Intuition is the ability to know, without words, to discern the truth about something without explanation. In other words, intuition is the ability to sense the answer to some problem without justifying that answer in some way or having to prove our conclusion. There is just a deep knowingness within us that we're on the right track, or that this is the way to go. It is the whisper of our loving God-self guiding us forward for our highest benefit.

When we use intuition to direct our lives, we find that:

1. *We know we are in the right place at the right time doing just what we need to be doing for our highest good.* For example, those of you who

have used your intuition to pick up this book and read it, may find that you get quite a lot out of it. Those of you who used logic to pick out this book, or are reading it because you feel you *should* read it, may find that you are disappointed, bored, or confused.

2. *Many doorways open for us, doorways we didn't even know existed.* For example, let's say that there's a big concert that you've been eager to attend, but you know it's been sold out for weeks. You've been wondering and wondering how you could possibly get tickets, and you've just about given up your search. One morning at work, you feel a sudden, strong urge to call up an old friend you haven't seen for a while and ask her out to lunch. She says, "Oh, I'd love to. I'm so glad you called. Maybe you could use these two extra tickets I have for this concert next week. . . ." As you can see, by following your intuition, you received something you might not have even thought possible. Tickets to a concert may seem like an insignificant issue, but it demonstrates the power of using that inner gut feeling in any one of thousands of situations, from simple and fun, to serious or critical.

3. *Our aspirations are realized more quickly.* Even if the realization of our goal seems far away, we can see great progress being made along the way. Using intuition causes our lives to flow smoothly and easily. Acting out of fear, logic, or guilt creates blockages and bumps in the road. For example, let's imagine that you've been working with a particular therapist for two years and that you're comfortable with him. Lately, though, you've been sensing that you have stopped learning, and you're feeling an urge to seek out another therapist with whom to work on your personal issues. However, instead of following this urge, you remain loyal to your first therapist because he's familiar to you and you're afraid to start over with someone

> new. Because of your decision, you may discover that the road to your therapist's office comes under construction and you have a long detour to get there. Or you may find that you begin to become irritable in your therapy sessions. Or perhaps you notice that you are generally more anxious or depressed.

In this example, the Universe is pointing out to you that there is a better way for you. There is no need to admonish yourself for taking the familiar road. When you discover that you have neglected your intuition, gently acknowledge this and move on in a more beneficial direction—the one that is silently tugging at you inside—the one that you "know" is right for you. Even if you are fearful at first, the God-Force will support you every step of the way. This is its desire, function and pleasure. The Universe loves you and has only your best interest at heart.

MYTHS

We live in a world in which scientific and technological knowledge is almost worshipped. After all, science and technology have allowed us to live longer lives and permitted our global economic systems to thrive. While this is positive and good for us, we often forget that there are other aspects of being human which need addressing, among them our mental health and well-being as individuals and as groups. Because scientific knowledge and technological expertise are so revered and so widely utilized for problem solving, the use of intuition can often be ridiculed. Stemming from this viewpoint are several myths involving the use of intuition to answer questions we have about work projects, people's actions, personal decisions, and the like. Many folks just don't believe in the power of intuition. Their influence on us can create inner blocks that lead us away from exercising our intuitive powers.

Some of the better-known myths about intuition are these:

1. Using intuition could get us into big trouble. Logic is at least provable and/or seeable.

2. Intuition is a feminine characteristic. It's not for men.

3. Intuition is used only when you're not smart enough to figure it all out for yourself.

4. Intuition is used as a last resort, when all else fails.

5. Using intuition is just another name for using "psychic" abilities.

To believe any of these or to listen to someone who considers these ideas to be accurate, is to hinder ourselves from tapping into and utilizing one of the most powerful gifts given to us by Divine creation.

The truer statements would be the following:

1. Subjective (inner, sensed) proof is more accurate than objective (outside, measurable) proof. Following our intuition can lead us where logic never could, even though we may need to use logic as a component of our problem-solving process. Something must *feel* right first, or we are headed for trouble.

2. The gift of intuition is given to all human beings, for we are all spiritual beings too, and intuition is a product of Divine Spirit. Some men may not have developed their intuitive sense as much as some women because of the masculine world's strong ties to science and technology and taboos regarding use of the emotions or inner senses. However, intuition can be developed through practice, regardless of gender.

3. Intuition has nothing to do with being intelligent or with the size of the brain. It is an *inner experience* of which every person has the opportunity to take advantage.

4. For problem solving, decision making, or investigation of any kind, seeking answers from Infinite Intelligence, and then tapping into and following one's intuition is the beginning of the process. This can be followed by the use of science, technology, or logic as inwardly directed.

5. Listening to our intuition is not about foretelling the future, delving into ours or other's past lives, communing with dead relatives, or reading someone's aura. The function of intuition is that it is a guide for living life more fully, successfully, and pleasurably. It is the voice of love that operates only for wellness, happiness, unity, and peace.

For many of us, and for me, the consequences of using our intuition and trusting it were experienced as painful when we grew up. Some of us weren't even aware that there was such a tool available to us, so it wouldn't have occurred to us to lead our lives in such a way. Still others of us are out of practice and have a difficult time discerning our intuitive voice. Whether we were influenced by others' judgment, unaware of intuition's power, or are presently out of practice, we now have the opportunity to begin living our lives intuitively and trusting the insightful strength of our inner knowingness. Just how to do that is our next subject of discussion.

TUNING IN TO GUT WISDOM

Becoming aware of our inner wisdom is actually quite simple. Following that gut feeling can be a bit more difficult, but both can be developed through practice. We begin by focusing on what we want to know. Remember, we create according to the thought energy we emit to the Universe. Therefore, whatever our problem, we start by asking Infinite Intelligence for answers. If this is done repeatedly, prayerfully, passionately, and from the heart, answers will eventually come to us in the form of insights, flashes, revelations such as "aha's," or strong urges. Although our hunch or gut feeling comes in the form of a thought or knowingness, something like a newspaper article, a street sign, a letter we receive in the mail, a line in a book, or something someone says, may also trigger an intuitive realization.

A caution here is that sometimes we may want a definite answer to something immediately and the Universe is not yet ready to divulge a solution. What Infinite Intelligence *will* do is to give us a next step toward the creation of our desire. Our degree of frustration hinges upon our ability to surrender our urgent need for resolution and upon our willingness to accept that we are in process. For example, we may feel frustrated when we are considering divorce and don't yet know whether to leave or stay. It is important to remember that decisions are merely products of sometimes lengthy processes and that there are lessons to be learned all along the way. If we do not get an intuitive hunch, it is wise to sit tight until something is made clear.

It is also important to note that we may feel confused as to which inner voice is that of intuition. We may hear several voices at once, each competing for our attention. The chief factor of which to be aware is that the voice of Divine Intelligence is generally very calm and tranquil, asserting itself with strong knowingness. Other thoughts inside of you may sound fearful or be laced with agitation or anxiety. Your true intuitive sensing is serene and peaceful. This holds true even if the follow-through carries with it some apprehension. As in our former example, if it is the right time to file for divorce, we will automatically know it, even if we feel a bit nervous about moving in that direction. When we are given an intuitive directive and we follow the instruction, the Universe backs us 100 percent, and we are given exactly what we need for all to flow smoothly.

Following our gut feelings is a question of trusting ourselves, even though we may have never learned that skill. There is no one who can possibly know what is right for us better than the Divine voice that lives within. As mentioned before, other people may think they know what we *should* do, but we are the only ones who can determine our best plan of action. Others may try to direct our lives out of concern for us or out of the need to control, but in the end, our healthiest response must always feel correct *within us*. There is no need to explain ourselves to anyone. We can quietly follow our own hearts, seeking encouragement from like-minded friends, teachers, or helping professionals if we lack support from significant others.

Learning to tune in to gut wisdom and then follow it is really a process of trial and error. The more we practice, the more we learn which of our responses are intuitive ones. If we carefully observe, we will find that when we abide by Divine inner direction, we will experience a surge of power and an abundance of resources. When we deny our inner voice, we may suffer scarcity of resources, confusion, anxiety, anger, or weakness. The latter is just the Universe attempting to pull us back on track. We must not admonish ourselves while learning. Rather, we must gently redirect ourselves until we feel a knowingness within our heart and contentment with our choice.

In summary, then, tuning in to gut wisdom requires the following few steps:

1. Focus on what you want to know.
2. Listen for your inner voice. Look for signs which may trigger that inner voice.
3. Follow your Divine inner direction.
4. Observe how this feels.
5. Practice, practice, practice.

Remember, your power lies within you and is yours for the asking. Using your intuition is a magical way to live and promises hope, peace, and greater happiness.

LEARNING THROUGH EXPERIENCE

A. *Contemplate the following questions:*

1. *Think of a time in your life when you followed your intuition. What was the outcome? How did you feel after following your gut? Did everything go smoothly? Bumpily? Recall the situation in all of its detail.*
2. *Think of a time in your life when you did something because you felt you should do it. What was the outcome? When compared to following your gut, did you notice any difference in the way everything worked out?*
3. *Think of a decision you need to make about something this week or month. What has your inner guidance been whispering (or even shouting) for you to do? This could be something small or big.*

B. *Guided Meditation*

Listening to and Trusting Inner Guidance

Close your eyes and relax. Take several slow, deep breaths, relaxing your body more and more with each exhalation. Now, imagine that your mind becomes as quiet as a peaceful lake. Be there for a few minutes until you feel tranquil and quiet, like the water.

When you feel relaxed, focus your conscious awareness on a deep place within your body where you feel that your intuition resides. This is the physical place where you can most easily contact your inner guide. When you have done that, pick a situation, a challenge or a problem in your life about which you would like to know more. You might want understanding, or perhaps you want to know your next step. You might desire to know in which direction to proceed or how to handle a difficult circumstance in a healthier way.

In your very relaxed state, ask your inner guide about this situation. The answers may come in words, feelings, or images. You will have a gut feeling or a knowingness about an answer that has come directly from your inner guide. Try not to be attached to an answer you want to hear. See if you can let go and accept the voice of your true inner wisdom.

Remember, if an answer does not immediately come, thank your intuitive self for listening, end your meditation and go about your life. The answers will come later, either from inside of you in the form of a feeling or an idea, or from outside through a person, a book, an event, a newspaper or magazine article, a street sign, or the like.

If you do get a gut feeling about something, see if you can summon the courage to act on it. If you can truly accept this answer and follow its direction, it will lead to greater aliveness and empowerment, and more opportunities will begin to open up for you.

Now, take a few more moments to listen in silence and see if you hear anything additional. When you are ready, express your appreciation to this part of you, slowly open your eyes and come back into the room.

C. *Try this exercise:*

Dialoguing

If you are right-handed, let your right hand denote your conscious, rational mind, and allow your left hand to denote your intuitive mind. If you are left-handed, reverse it.

Write down a simple question that is of importance to you with your dominant hand. Then, without thinking, begin to answer it with your other hand. Just let the words flow out through your fingers. This may feel difficult, for you may feel like you're in kindergarten again. However, it doesn't matter what the letters look like. Just continue on. Get a dialogue going, and keep it going as long as it feels appropriate. You may be surprised at what you learn.

This can also be done on the computer or by sitting alternately in two different chairs and talking to yourself. Decide which chair represents the rational mind and which one the Divine intuitive mind. Remember to let your words flow without thinking about them too hard.

Example:

Right Hand: I don't like my job. I think I should look for a new one. I don't know where to look.

Left Hand: Maybe it's not the right time for you to change jobs. Why do you hate your job?

Right Hand: It's my boss. He's so critical of me.

Left Hand: Maybe the problem isn't the job, but how you react to your boss's criticism.

Right Hand: He makes me so angry!

Left Hand: What about that book Mary showed you in the book store about dealing with difficult people? It might be good for you.

Etc., etc.

Do all the good you can,
By all the means you can,
In all the ways you can,
At all the times you can,
To all the people you can,
As long as ever you can.
—John Wesley

CHAPTER 11

The Gift of Service

ONE of the great antidotes to life's harshness is the gift of service. When we're down and out, we tend to isolate ourselves from the world, cocooning ourselves until we feel better. We may need to spend time alone for a while, but it is to our benefit to recognize that we possess the power to counteract difficult circumstances with a simple choice to serve. In the early nineties I had an experience that demonstrated to me the power of service to mend our minds and hearts.

I was just beginning my career as a psychotherapist and struggling with my sense of adequacy as a counselor, when I joined the board of a start-up hunger agency. The organization was to pick up usable, leftover food from restaurants, grocery stores, food warehouses, and the like in order to deliver it to soup kitchens. At the time, we had no funds; we were just a group of enthusiastic individuals wanting to make a difference. As a founding member, I was given the opportunity to appear on television and talk about the agency's mission. The program, airing at 7:00 a.m. on two consecutive weekend mornings, we thought, would be seen by very few people, but, optimistically, we went ahead and did it anyway.

To our surprise, the next day we received a call from an elderly woman. When I answered her call, her voice shook on the phone as she told me that she had a substantial donation for the agency. She then asked if I would come downtown (where she lived in an old hotel in a poor neighborhood) to pick up her check. I set up a time that our driver and I could go there because it sounded as if this was the only way we would receive the money. She didn't want to put the check in the mail because she was afraid it would get lost.

The day soon arrived, and our driver and I headed for the hotel. When we approached her room, the door creaked open, and standing there was a frail and emaciated old woman. She asked us to come in, and in the thirty minutes that followed, we found out that she had lived in this run-down hotel for many years in a tiny, single room with a bed, a TV, a small dresser, and a round table with two chairs. She never went out except occasionally to go to the doctor. She was paying a woman to bring her food each day, but the lady was keeping most of the money and bringing back only meager portions of food. Basically, this sweet old woman was starving to death. When we explained to her that our charity could not service her directly, she said she understood. To our astonishment, she proceeded to write out a hearty check (which turned out to be good) to the agency, anyway.

The driver and I were appalled at her condition and immediately went out to buy a fresh lunch for her as well as some staples that she could keep on hand. When we brought the food back to her, her eyes lit up like those of a three-year-old child opening her birthday presents. She couldn't believe anyone would want to help her the way we did.

As upset as I was at the whole situation, I have never in my life felt my heart so full. The driver and I were thankful for the large dollar donation to our organization, but the real joy came from what we did for this woman. We were truly given the greatest of gifts—the ability to give of ourselves, and nothing could bring greater peace and joy than that! Thoughts of any inadequacy disappeared in that moment, replaced by calm satisfaction, increased motivation to help the hungry, and the memory of that woman's smile.

We all have the ability to give of ourselves, and it need not be done in such a dramatic way. When we are down and out or feeling weary, depressed, afraid, or irritated, we can remember our natural core of love. All it takes is a decision to be of service to somebody—a choice that is always available to us. No matter how small the act, we will reap the rewards immediately, brightening the light within us and around us.

With that said, and simple though it may seem, the concept of service is not complete without a thorough look at the finer points that arise as we attempt to be of assistance. To obtain a complete understanding of service, how to motivate ourselves to reach out and how to be helpful in the most beneficial manner, is to ensure the promise of greater happiness to all parties involved. Therefore, the following sections address a greater comprehension of the principles of service and how to use this gift most advantageously.

GIVING AND RECEIVING

One of the great motivational factors regarding service is the realization that when we give, we also receive, as shown in the example above. When we give of ourselves unconditionally, the act of giving becomes a gift to both the recipient and to ourselves as well. Why does this occur? Its truth can be seen when we view humanity as a whole.

Humanity is a bonded and merged collection of souls, all sharing the same essence. For underneath the uniqueness of our physical features lies the universal life force energy of which we have spoken. This energy is invisible and lacks the material substance, which seems to keep us separate on a physical plane. In reality, though, we are all connected. We are fundamentally joined together, rather than distinct entities. Therefore, to give to another necessarily means giving to oneself. What is given out always comes back to its source.

What about giving to ourselves? Many of us have been taught that to be good people, we must be selfless or avoid thinking about ourselves. This notion is as far from the truth as possible. Are we not one of the interconnected souls of humanity? What would happen if we denied ourselves and our needs? When we neglect ourselves, we actually affect the whole. This does not mean to become overly self-indulgent; rather, it suggests that we should be attentive to our own needs as they arise, so that we may be at our best for others. On airplanes, mothers of small children are advised, in the case of emergency, to supply oxygen to themselves and *then* to their children. The same applies to all service-oriented activity, for what good are we to others if we are falling apart?

How can we discriminate between being of service to others and making the choice to take care of ourselves? The answer can only be found within. Following our intuitive urges will always lead us in the ideal direction. Our inner voice is always guiding us if only we will listen. We must become aware of any thoughts stemming from fear, those "I should" thoughts that impel us to do something for someone else even though it may not feel right at the moment. There will always be a perfect time for servicing others and a perfect time for servicing ourselves. We need merely follow our inner guidance and we will know.

How about those times when we offer ourselves to someone who has trouble receiving our gift? It might help to know that love is always felt, even if on a subconscious level, but that generally, the Universe will redirect us to someone who can receive our gifts more fully. If a pitcher is throwing a baseball and there is no catcher, it becomes too difficult to carry out the activity. In such a case, the cycle of giving and receiving is broken, which is out of alignment with universal purpose. The same holds true for anyone attempting to provide service for another. When the intended recipient is unable to receive what is offered, inner guidance will redirect the giver's energy to another beneficiary until the Universe's objective is fulfilled. Thus, again, it is always important for us to tune in to our intuitive inclinations, which point us in a more appropriate direction.

On the other hand, what if we are the one who has trouble receiving from others? Some of us may feel guilty when others are offering to help us, or we may not feel we deserve to receive good. Perhaps being on the receiving end triggers disturbing feelings of weakness or neediness. Whatever the reason, we must remember that our ability and willingness to receive offers others the opportunity to feel the peace and contentment that service can bring. When we deny them this chance, we hurt both of us. Keep in mind that this applies only in situations in which another is giving to us unconditionally and intuitively, not out of their own guilt or fear. In the latter circumstance, we generally feel their lack of integrity and may naturally refuse the offering.

It is also significant to note that we cannot be giving something without receiving and vice versa. Giving and receiving go hand in hand. Sometimes we may feel purely like the giver—the strong, wise, or competent one, silently judging the other person for being needy, fragile, or weak. Sometimes we may only think that we are the receiver, quietly chastising ourselves for being in this position. It is helpful to understand that in every interaction we are both the giver and the receiver.

A good example of this can be seen in the work of a psychotherapist. Classically, we might view a psychotherapist as the giver and a client as the receiver. But if we look closer, we realize that the psychotherapist may be giving expertise, nurturance, wisdom, and education, but that the psychotherapist is also receiving money, feelings of self-worth, skill practice, and fulfillment. In the same manner, the client is giving all the items that the therapist is receiving and receiving all the items that the therapist is giving. In that way, we comprehend that we are equals rather than either one of us being better than the other. When this can occur, greater peace is felt all around

TRUE GIVING

Giving of ourselves can produce great inner peace, or it can be accompanied by ambivalence, frustration, or disgust. It can create harmony and fulfillment or it can work to cause conflict or discord. Most of the time, giving is good for us and produces wonderful results. However, at times, our experience may prove to be something less than desirable. What's the difference? How can we be sure that our actions will generate peacefulness?

True, authentic service is the giving of ourselves with absolutely no expectations, demands, or thought of reward. This is better known as giving unconditionally and is the only kind of service that produces feelings of wellness, contentment, and pleasure. We've been taught in our fear-based world that others should do as much for us as we do for them, and furthermore, that we *need* this to happen in order to guarantee our happiness. I've witnessed couples keeping score, more focused on what they don't get rather than on what they do get or on what they can give. When this occurs, both parties suffer miserably, and the good that service could bring about gets lost in our expectation of being compensated for the good deed given.

The falsehood that needs addressing here is the notion that we need others to perform in a certain way in order to make us happy. The greater truth is that we each already have what we need inside of ourselves to create satisfaction and even joy. This comes in the form of our ability to open our hearts and reach out in love, whether that love is given to others or ourselves. Demands and expectations of returned kindness only block our capacity to reap the true rewards that come from giving unconditionally.

A student of mine once shared with me that her widowed father was highly critical of her and often irritable. Her dad was elderly and needed care, so my student would frequently buy him groceries and other items he required in the hope that her father would treat her differently. When nothing changed, the young lady became totally frustrated and enraged at her father's behavior. We worked for some time with her anger until she was ready to let it go. When she finally accepted the fact that he was old, cranky, and afraid, she made a conscious choice to continue helping him—this time without expectations that he change. Not only did she feel better, but her dad seemed to become less grumpy and critical. It seems that on some level he could now feel her genuine love for him and her desire to assist him. When he became cranky or judgmental, she was able to brush it off quickly and continue giving in this new unconditional way.

It is significant to note that giving unconditionally does not rule out boundary setting. Clients and students have asked me repeatedly about service to children who definitely need boundaries set in order to become healthy, integrated, and fully functioning adults. To give unconditionally to a child merely means that we eliminate judgment from our thoughts and communication. We still hold them accountable for their poor behavior, but we refrain from conveying that they are "bad" for acting in a certain way. We may even attempt to have conversation around their reasons for their conduct, making sure to listen nonjudgmentally to their answers. Nevertheless, true giving involves the ability to let go of the outcome to our demands while providing the appropriate consequences for their behavior. If we can look upon our kids as young people (souls) who are learning, growing, and evolving just like us, we can forgive their poor behavior while establishing healthy rules and regulations for living.

Setting boundaries applies to adults, too, but every situation is different and each one calls upon us to ask ourselves what unconditional giving would look like in such a circumstance. When there is confusion, it is always a good idea to check with our inner guidance, which will direct us to clarity in one way or another. The main point is to understand that if we are attempting to get something back through our giving efforts, we may prevent our own happiness from unfolding. The most valuable concept to keep in mind is that true service is made of love and comes from the heart. When anything else falls into the mix, we create inner and outer conflict. Authentic giving carries with it compassion, understanding, and a genuine desire to be of assistance.

TYPES OF SERVICE

When we think of the words *service* or *giving*, what generally comes to mind is a reaching out to someone in need in order to help him/her in some way. This most frequently occurs in the form of using words or actions to convey nurturance. This often works well and is a source of comfort for both the giver and receiver, which we have already discussed. However, there are times when our giving is outright rejected, or only partially successful, and rather than do nothing, we can be aware that there are other options available if they feel intuitively correct. Sometimes if we just tweak our form of giving, we can accomplish far more good. Below are listed some types of service that can prove to be highly useful in many situations.

1. We may not realize it, but *setting an example for others* can be potent teaching as well as a method of giving valuable and inspiring aid to another. Even if it appears that the other party is not receiving anything, modeling constructive behavior plants seeds in the consciousness of the viewer. We all learn as children to watch our parents, and we pick up many of our mannerisms from them. If love and kindness are modeled, it is absorbed on some level, and its effects are deeply felt. What adds power to modeling loving behavior is that it triggers an innate memory of our most natural state of being.

2. We are being of service just by *working on healing ourselves.* As we become more accepting, peaceful, and loving, we automatically offer

this to others. We can give out only what we already have inside, so the more we heal, the more fully we can be present and empathetic with others.

3. *Extending nonverbal, uplifting energy* is another way to give of ourselves. Examples of this include praying for another person, visualizing someone being happy and peaceful, imagining the other party receiving exactly what they want or need, and sending love or light silently to another. There are numerous variations on these mental techniques, and all represent a valuable means of creating harmony and/or positively affecting someone's behavior.

4. We can *share our own experience* with others if they are open to hearing us. To be successful here, we must refrain from giving advice or preaching to another. To merely share our experience means to use "I" language and to remain unattached to the other person following suit. If we can do this, we discover one of the most nonthreatening and rewarding ways to give of ourselves. Much education and vision can be communicated in this manner.

5. We can *help others to find their own answers by listening to their own inner guidance*. We do this by asking open-ended questions, allowing another to explore his/her own mind and heart. That is one of the most influential ways to serve, since eliciting someone's inner resources demonstrates the power that already lies within, providing increased self-confidence and empowerment. Information that is received in this way is remembered longer and acted on more quickly and efficiently.

LEARNING THROUGH EXPERIENCE

A. *Consider the following questions. As usual, journal your answers, discuss with someone in whom you can confide, or sit in silence for a short time while you contemplate your answers.*

1. *Think of a situation in which you see yourself mainly as the giver. What might you also be receiving here?*
2. *Think of a situation in which you see yourself mainly as the receiver. What might you also be giving here?*
3. *Think of a time when you gave something to someone because you felt you "should." How did that feel?*
4. *Think of a time you did something for someone because it felt intuitively correct. How did that feel?*
5. *When was the last time you did something for someone? Did you expect anything in return? If so, how did it feel? If not, how did that feel?*
6. *Have you ever had the experience of giving with no expectation, demand, or reward? Imagine that situation in all of its detail. How did it feel?*
7. *Think of one thing you could do this week that would increase your capacity to give or receive more fully. Make a commitment to put it into action.*

B. *Below are some ideas for giving to others. Pick one of these or make up your own and make it happen! See how it feels.*

1. *Volunteer for an organization that helps the homeless and hungry, deals with saving the planet, works with troubled kids, battered women, AIDS victims, cancer victims, premature babies, or the like. There are thousands of nonprofit agencies needing volunteer help.*
2. *Take flowers to a neighbor, friend, or relative.*
3. *Play a silly game with your child.*
4. *Soften your voice when you speak to people.*
5. *Invite someone over for dinner or send a card to someone.*
6. *Give someone a hug and tell him you love him.*
7. *Give a friend in need a ride or accompany her to a doctor's appointment.*
8. *Spend a day helping out in a nursing home.*
9. *Call someone you haven't talked to for awhile and say hello.*

You can explore the Universe looking
for somebody who is more deserving of your
love and affection than yourself and
you will not find that person anywhere.

—source unknown

CHAPTER 12

Loving Ourselves

WHEN I gaze upon my life, if there's one issue with which I've most struggled, it's been that of loving myself. For me, this manifested in shyness, fear of rejection, anxiety at being in front of a group, jealousy of others' successes, and an obsession with dieting. For many years it seemed no matter what I did, it wasn't good enough. There was still more I could accomplish, I'd tell myself, and I'd drive myself to the brink of exhaustion running after the elusive self-acceptance I so longed for. If only I were intelligent enough and productive enough, I could have approved of myself the way my father would have. If only I were thin enough and socially adept enough, I could compliment myself as my mother would have.

The trouble was, the "me" I yearned to be just didn't stick around for long. I might feel acceptable for a short while, basking in relief that I'd "made it," and in the next minute, hour or day I'd be confronted with the other "me," the one who was emotional, afraid, angry, bored, lazy, or sad. There was always someone brighter, kinder, steadier, stronger, or more capable, talented, or skillful. I compared myself to others no matter where I went, either placing myself above, or more often, below my object of contrast. I was full of self-judgment, which could be triggered at a moment's notice.

Through time, as I worked on resolving this matter and observing my own and other's behaviors, I realized that I wasn't very different from the clients I counseled, the students I taught, the businessmen I encountered, the friends I had, the store clerks who helped me, the politicians in our midst, the celebrities about whom I'd read, or the clergymen and women of all different religions. I came to understand that in our humanness, we each have others to whom we compare ourselves, and inner strivings that aren't yet met. I came to recognize that this sense of self-condemnation seems to be found everywhere to greater or lesser degrees. Whether someone is a criminal or a prominent statesman, he usually possesses a need to be more or to be better, terrible remorse over how she has behaved at one time or another, or hidden self-rage for characteristics that feel unacceptable.

Granted, this may manifest in some disguised fashion, so as to fool us, but nevertheless, self-recrimination exists more often than we might think. Some people I've known act bitter and irritable, some sugary sweet, and others remain mad at the world, unaware of the real cause of their discomfort. Some individuals become workaholics, alcoholics, or shop-aholics to deaden self-deprecatory thoughts and the anxiety and/or depression this kind of thinking fosters. Whether we are aware or unaware of our self-judgments, they seem to exist in our fear-based world, even though the powerful antidotes of acceptance, forgiveness, compassion, and love wait patiently to be put to use when we are ready.

How has this come to be? What is the nature of self-recrimination? How do we recover? What follows are some thoughts on these subjects.

SOCIETAL IMPACTS

We live in a culture in which our waking consciousness is most commonly fear-based. We see ourselves as separate from each other and separate from God, not realizing that our safety would be guaranteed, should we remember our true nature—that of lovingness, unity, and grace. Because we fear being alone and uncared for, we strive to draw attention to ourselves, assuring ourselves that someone will spot us and therefore, remain connected to us. We, as a society, have devised a multitude of ways to do this and each of us is trained by our parents, teachers, and the media to act in such a way that we are noticed, accepted, and commended. Much of the time we fall short of society's expectations, which further intensifies our fears and causes us to criticize and denounce ourselves.

Tara Brach, renowned author, psychologist, and lecturer, calls this the "trance of unworthiness," which she states is part of the human condition in Western society. She says it clearly in the following excerpt from her book, *Radical Acceptance:*

> *We learn early in life that any affiliation—with family and friends, at school or in the workplace—requires proving that we are worthy. We are under pressure to compete with each other, to get ahead, to stand out as intelligent, attractive, capable, powerful, wealthy.... We must overcome our flaws by controlling our bodies, controlling our emotions, controlling our natural surroundings, controlling other people. And we must strive tirelessly—working, acquiring, consuming, achieving, e-mailing, over-committing, and rushing—in a never-ending quest to prove ourselves once and for all.*

What a fear-based society can't know is that we are already connected to each other—that we all have our human (lower self) flaws, but that at our core we are all loving, creative, and talented individuals, each emanating from the Divine Mind, each full of beauty, and each capable of more than we could possibly imagine. Our worth isn't to be found in the gods of society—money, power, prestige, looks, awards, grades, the perfect marriage, or any other ideals that we have set as our standards for achievement. Our worth is a given, and in our connection to each other through our innate Divine energy, we find that we are all a part of a loving whole, whether our lower self personalities reflect that or not.

Living, however, in a culture that breeds self-doubt and self-recrimination, the messages are so strong that we find ourselves immersed in mistaken perceptions of what is true and what is not. As we work toward moving in the direction of love-consciousness, we need the help of others who have traveled this road and a recommitment to use all of the available resources, which rectify any erroneous mainstream thought. To rediscover our true, natural being requires a retraining of our minds, and this necessitates time spent with spiritual books, tapes or classes, meditation, contemplation, and the like. The reeducation process is accessible and obtainable for those of us who are dedicated and steadfast about our growth, even if we have to recommit ourselves over and over again.

During the process of working to transform our self-perceptions, we are certain to tap into those inner reservoirs of self-loathing or self-criticism. Examining the nature of guilt and shame as well as the consequences of such emotional states can help us to understand and overcome such conditions and catalyze greater self-acceptance.

GUILT, SHAME, AND PROJECTION

Guilt and shame are two powerful emotions that wreak havoc inside of us, causing much suffering and discontent. When we are lost in self-judgment, one of these is usually at play and, unless we understand the mechanism by which they get their power and the results that follow, we may have great difficulty in letting them go.

What is guilt? Guilt is all of the "should haves," "would haves," and "if only's" that are part of our thought vocabulary. Guilt deals with past regrettable actions, thoughts, and feelings, and is fueled by the hindsight as to how we thought we should have done something. In guilt, we feel as if we made a mistake for which we condemn ourselves.

Some of the fears that might arise during guilty moments are:

1. I'm afraid I might get caught.
2. I'm worried what you might think of me if you find out.
3. I'm afraid I'll have to come out of denial.
4. I'm afraid of not liking myself.
5. I'm afraid of the repercussions of this behavior.

Some of the surrounding feelings might be:

1. I feel naughty.
2. I feel anxious.
3. I feel depressed.
4. I feel sad.
5. I feel embarrassed.

Various thoughts that might go through our heads are:

1. I hope nobody finds out!
2. I shouldn't/should have done that.
3. If only I could have acted that way!
4. If only I had said that, he would have been nicer to me.
5. I should call my sister.

Are any of these familiar to you?

Shame is an amplification of guilt in that we have intensified our guilt or guilty behaviors to the point of deciding that we *are* our mistakes and therefore are "damaged goods." Shame has to do with our personhood instead of one behavior and has the power to block us from living fully, stop us from pursuing our dreams, or devastate us entirely.

Some of the fears that might be triggered when we feel ashamed are:

1. Fear of failure
2. Fear of abandonment
3. Fear of emotional pain
4. Fear of not being loved
5. Fear of humiliation
6. Fear of losing our job
7. Fear no one will hire me again

Some of the feelings associated with shame are:

1. I feel stupid.
2. I feel little and weak.
3. I feel helpless.
4. I feel out of control.
5. I feel paranoid, like everyone is watching and judging me.
6. I feel dishonor.
7. I feel disgrace.

Thoughts that might be upsetting us when we feel ashamed are:

1. I want to die.
2. I can't stand the pain.
3. I'm terrified.
4. I'm no good.
5. I'm such an awful person.
6. I'm an idiot!
7. I'm so bad!

Do any of these sound typical of you? Of anyone you know? If shame is not a frequent occurrence in your life, have you ever felt that way?

In our culture we frequently have experiences such as these, however unconscious they may be at times. When we are not consciously aware that guilt and shame are ruling our minds, and that our self-recriminating thoughts are running rampant, we often project onto others the faults that we have assigned to ourselves. Frequently it is easier to blame others than to blame ourselves. When we project blame onto others, we can avoid the pain, which arises from self-condemnation. What is really happening is that we are treating other people just as we treat ourselves. We just don't realize that the cause of our discomfort stems from inside of us, and can only be remedied by becoming aware of guilty or shameful thoughts, forgiving ourselves, and holding compassion for our humanness.

Whenever we find ourselves angry at or critical of others, we are in a state of projection, and must work to uncover the underlying cause, which is self nonacceptance in some form. Once we can see where the real cause lies, we can move in a direction of real healing, which is the subject of our next section.

THE ROAD TO RECOVERY

The path to loving ourselves fully can be a long, arduous one, perhaps even the task of a lifetime, or more. However, great strides can be made in short periods of time, just by making the commitment and setting the intention to practice greater awareness and to entertain the idea that we are each doing the best we can with what we know at this point in our evolution. Accepting ourselves where we are is a mantra we can carry with us, day in and day out. There simply is no right or wrong place to be. We are merely where Infinite Intelligence wants us to be, learning from all that occurs, so that we can remember who we are and operate out of our natural goodness. As we work to uncover and replace the self-deprecatory thoughts that often control our minds, we begin to sense a freedom unlike any other we've tasted before.

This effort toward self nonjudgment and acceptance can take many forms, many of which we have discussed previously. Using our tools such as prayer, meditation, contemplation, affirmation, and psycho-spiritual education and support, are as essential to the process as brushing our teeth is to oral hygiene. Several exercises at the end of this chapter are designed to help us break self-discriminatory patterns of thought and perception, and can prove to be quite useful during this process, particularly if they are repeated in some sort of continual fashion. I'd encourage full exploration and repetition of these exercises when time is available.

However, I'd like to spend a moment here on one of the most powerful means to bring self-acceptance into our lives on a more frequent basis. That is the use of "insight" meditation or "mindfulness" meditation, which you may recall from chapter 8.

We begin with the understanding that we can alter only that of which we are aware. Many of our beliefs and perceptions lie hidden somewhere in our subconscious mind and must be retrieved through the conscious effort to examine our thoughts and feelings in order to effect a change. This is difficult to do while engaged in living with its outer distractions. Therefore, it helps to begin with silent practice sessions—perhaps no more than twenty minutes per day if time is tight.

The idea is to observe what is within our minds, then work to respond nonjudgmentally to what we see. Acceptance of every thought, feeling and belief is our choice to make, and holding the intention to make that choice, even when we fall short, is our task.

Thus, we sit comfortably in silence in a place in which we will not be disturbed, and we begin by watching our breath, just being aware of the rising and falling of our breath. We use this as our center point to which we return whenever we are able. Remembering that it is natural for our minds to drift, we allow ourselves to observe the contents of where the mind has wandered without judging. When working on self-acceptance, we're looking for self-critical thoughts and just allowing them to be there. We can then view ourselves with compassion, for we know that it feels uncomfortable to be self-critical. We might ask ourselves where these thoughts come from and choose to love the little child inside that struggles with this self-view. We might create new kind-hearted phrases to feed ourselves instead of the older, more condemning ones, or we might note the relationship of our thoughts to sensations inside of our physical body, again without judgment. The amazing thing that happens when we surround our thoughts and feelings with acceptance and compassion is that many of our self-deprecatory thoughts merely fall away and lose their power over us.

Thus, if I were practicing, it might sound like this inside of me. Keep in mind that some of what follows is merely awareness, not actual thoughts, but for our purposes here, it is written in words, as though I were hearing all of it.

Breathing, rising, falling ... rising, falling ... rising, falling ... (memory) Carol was nasty to me this morning ... tightness in chest ... Okay, let it be ... I hate this feeling ... Oh well, so you hate this feeling ... I'm so angry with her ... You're just having a human feeling ... Why does she treat me that way? ... She's so critical of me!... Oh yeah, maybe I'm just critical of myself ... I wish I could love myself more ... Oh well, you are where you are and that's okay ... Breathing, rising, falling ...rising, falling ... rising falling ... I need to spend more time with David ... I don't do enough for him or anyone else ...Oh yeah, I'm in my critical self ... Okay, it's all right to be there; that's what you learned from Dad ... Breathing, rising, falling... rising, falling ... rising, falling ... rising, falling ... rising, falling ... Feeling anxious ... What's that about?... I have so much work to do, I don't know when I'm going to fit it all in ... the bills, all those errands, that computer work, returning all those phone calls ... slow down, Laurie ... I can't, I'm nervous; my stomach's in knots ... I can't stand that I'm this way ... It's okay, Laurie; whatever you're experiencing now is okay. I'm so sorry you have to feel this way ... I love you no matter what you get done and no matter how you feel ... Breathing, rising, falling ... rising, falling ... rising, falling ...

If I were to continue this with acceptance of every inner experience, I would be teaching myself to respond to all circumstances more calmly and compassionately. After awhile, awareness would become a greater part of my waking consciousness, and I would be teaching myself that I'm human and doing the best I can with what I know at all times.

For those of you who resist being nonjudgmental toward yourselves, you may want to think about what it is you get out of beating up on yourself. Often there is a hidden payoff for belittling ourselves, and examining what it might be can be an important step toward letting it go. In addition, many students tell me that they can't possibly accept some of their behaviors because they don't believe such behaviors are acceptable. This is a perfect opportunity to explore where they got that notion and its validity. We generally believe what we've been taught, and we must remember that our teachers were human also, and had limited vision of actual reality just like us. It is valuable to recall that we have choices in the present time. To judge ourselves harshly is a choice which causes suffering. To accept ourselves fully is a choice that brings about peace and comfort, which every human being deserves.

In conclusion, learning to love ourselves is a process, one that may be continuous throughout life. However, there is much that we can do to speed up the process and calm those internal critical voices and beliefs. When we pay attention, become more aware, and make new nonjudgmental choices, we can calm our inner turbulence and create a more relaxed and tranquil existence.

LEARNING THROUGH EXPERIENCE

A. *Explore the following questions:*

1. *Do you ever feel as though you are living in a "trance of unworthiness," such as Tara Brach describes? If so, under what circumstances, particularly?*
2. *What do you feel guilty about, if anything? Who taught you to feel guilty, and through what means?*
3. *What do you feel ashamed of, if anything? Who taught you to feel ashamed, and through what means?*
4. *Are you more of a "blame myself" kind of person, or a "blame others" kind of person? Think of a time when you might have projected anger on another when you were really angry with yourself. For what might you have been angry with yourself?*
5. *Try twenty minutes of mindfulness meditation and discuss with a friend afterwards, or journal your experiences. Ask yourself these questions associated with your meditation:*
    a. *Was I resistant to accepting my thoughts and feelings fully? If so, what might have been my payoff?*
    b. *Do I feel deserving of loving myself completely? If not, where does that belief come from?*
    c. *Who were my primary teachers as a child? How did they feel about themselves?*

B. *Guided Meditation: Self-Loving*

As usual, you may record this and play it back to yourself, or you may read paragraph by paragraph, closing your eyes to visualize between readings.

Close your eyes and begin to breathe deeply and slowly, placing your awareness on your breath and finding a rhythm that is perfect for you—in and out—slowly, completely, and deeply. Feel the tension move out of you with each exhalation and feel your body relax more extensively with each breath. Feel yourself sinking into relaxation … peace … calm, as though you are riding an elevator down, down and further down.

When you are comfortable, imagine that you see in front of you seven marble stairs. Begin to walk toward the stairs … Now you are at the top of the stairs. Begin your descent down each step and continue until you are standing at the bottom. At this point you see a door in front of you. Notice what the door looks like. Take note of all its details … Now push the door open and go through it. On the other side is a large room in which you see many clones of yourself. These clones represent the many parts of you—the parts you love and the parts which you do not love or approve of. Look around and identify as many parts of you as you can. You may, for example, see the "angry" you or the "sad" you or the "happy, joyous" you or the you that is "lonely." At any rate, identify as many loved parts of you as you can, and then notice the unloved parts of you.

When you have had sufficient time to do this, make a large circle with all the parts of you that you love. Take note again of all these parts of you that you love. Feel proud, feel grateful, feel all the affection and admiration you have inside you well up and flow freely through you.

Now see all the other parts you have left out of your circle—the parts of you of which you are ashamed—the parts that are unaccepted, the parts that are unloved—the parts of you that you even hate or about which you feel guilty. Motion these parts to enter inside the circle. Make sure that they all come into the center of the circle. When they are all inside, see the loved parts all join hands and move inward so that they enclose the not-so-loved parts tightly, lovingly, tenderly. See your loved parts caring compassionately for the unloved parts and allowing them to know that they are completely acceptable—helping them to realize that being human means possessing a variety of qualities, including ones like them. Let them know that from now on they will be loved and supported and not cast out for any reason. Let them know that all human beings have qualities like them. Let yourself realize that through love and acceptance of these parts of you that you will be more able to manifest the loved parts of you. Know completely that it is through acceptance, forgiveness, and nonjudgment that we find peace. Repeat this statement to yourself: it is through acceptance, forgiveness and nonjudgment that we find peace.

When you are ready, move back toward the door and then leave through the same opening. Now climb up the seven marble stairs and begin to bring your attention back to your meditation area. Slowly move your feet, your hands … stretch a little and then a little more. When you feel ready, open your eyes and be here.

C. *Affirmations for loving ourselves: Pick two to three of these at one time and say them as if you believe them, ten times in the morning, ten times at night, and ten times in the middle of the day. Whenever you are down on yourself, think, "cancel, cancel," and substitute your affirmation(s).*

- *I am loveable and capable.*
- *I am a unique and priceless person with a lot to offer.*
- *I am a valuable and important person, worthy of respect.*
- *I am a radiant being filled with light and love.*

- *I love myself fully just the way I am. I am enough.*
- *I am kind, compassionate, and gentle with myself.*
- *I feel warm and loving toward myself, for I am a unique and precious being, ever doing the best my awareness allows.*
- *As I love myself more, I have more to give others.*
- *I count my blessings and rejoice in my growing awareness.*
- *I now approve of all my actions.*
- *I am trusting myself and going at my own speed.*
- *No matter what you do or say to me, I am still a worthwhile person.*

D. *Activity: Celebrating You!*

Make a list of all the parts of you that you like. Make a poster with pictures or words depicting who you are and what's unique and beautiful about you. Make it colorful and fun to look at. Put this poster in a place where you will see it each day. If you can't think of anything to put on the poster, ask a friend or someone who cares about you to give you ideas.

Your task is not to seek for love,
but merely to seek and find all the
barriers within yourself that
you have built against it.
—Rumi

Chapter 13

Coping with Strong Emotions

I'VE often thought of myself as "the Queen of emotions," because of my extreme sensitivity. Growing up, I would often find myself in tears over seemingly small incidents, or enraged when someone wasn't treated fairly. Many things scared me, and I coped with long bouts of childhood depression and loneliness. The difficulty with this was that it was painful, and my ability to steady and transcend these emotional states developed more slowly than I would have liked. However, I was determined to create a new reality for myself, and I worked hard to learn all I could from this darkness within me. Thus, along the way, I uncovered a good deal of natural wisdom that was just waiting to be discovered, the same natural wisdom that resides within each one of us.

As the quote above so aptly states, I found that the loving state of mind is always present, even if hidden. The obstacles in its way of manifesting are the learned fears that we have acquired over time, erroneous perceptions of what is real. When we acknowledge and release those feelings, we are free to remember who and what we really are—beings of love. We also open ourselves to the knowledge that we can be safe and protected in a world that often looks dangerous. This safety comes to us through the power of the God-Force, for when we reconnect with Infinite Intelligence, we can find purpose, meaning, and compassionate presence in all that happens to us and to others.

No doubt you have experienced your share of raw emotion. As we discussed in chapter 4, we all have our ups and our downs, and our "gullies" can be filled with deep gloom and shadows of all shapes and sizes. Even if your emotional life hasn't been as intense as mine, the human condition dictates that each of us has our hurdles to overcome. For some of us, strong emotions can cause much suffering, pain, and sorrow. In this chapter, we address some of the specific emotional states in the attempt to get a better handle on coping with them. Keep in mind that our basic tools from chapters 8 and 9 can be developed and utilized when striving to manage even the most difficult of emotional states. As a matter of fact, intense feelings can increase our faith and help us to master the skills we've discussed previously. Spiritual reading, prayer, meditation, contemplation, affirmation, present momenting, acceptance, expression of feelings, seeking support, surrender, gratitude, and positive focusing are foundational tools that are always available to us and can be cultivated though time. Here, we endeavor to look more deeply into each of several emotional states in the attempt to understand them more completely and therefore, cope in an improved manner with their appearance in our lives.

Before moving on, however, it is significant to discuss the use of medication. Sometimes, when emotions are very strong, certain chemicals in our brain fall below the level of function that is therapeutically required to be helpful and constructive. It's as though we become frozen in our emotional states, unable to move forward, stuck in survival mode. Work with a therapist may become stagnant, and learning new material may be quite difficult.

This happened to me at times in my past, and being "alternative-medicine/holistic-minded," I felt that medicine was some kind of evil, foreign substance, which might harm me. In addition, with the stigma that society places on mental illness, it was not easy to admit that I was having such difficulties. It was not until I cried uncontrollably when my father was ill with lung cancer, that two of my psychotherapist colleagues convinced me to make an appointment with a psychiatrist and get the medical help I needed. With the use of an anti-depressant, I was able to move more easily through that challenging period of time and learn from it. I realized that medicine can be a gift from God and that we all deserve to receive the help that is offered by the Universe, if it is appropriate to our condition and prescribed by a knowledgeable physician.

That is not to say that there are not many wonderfully useful complementary, more natural methods available to address intense emotional states. Herbal therapy, homeopathy, flower essences, light therapy, and improved nutrition are sample modalities that have helped to balance moods and influence the chemistry of the brain. The caution here is to work with well-informed and experienced health practitioners who can monitor progress and oversee treatment. Often these methods can be utilized in conjunction with prescription drug therapy, if necessary, and may allow for lower dosages than would otherwise be needed.

Keeping this in mind, we move on to a discussion of some of the more common emotional states that can threaten our peace of mind, keep us stuck, or create havoc within our relationships.

FEAR

Fear is the father of all destructive emotions, for whenever we feel troubled in any way, fear is involved. As humans, we often feel fear of success, failure, rejection, abandonment, impoverishment, death, life, and of physical and emotional pain. When considering all other uncomfortable emotional states, one of these fears is usually underneath, even though we may be unaware of its existence at the time. At its extreme, fear can become *panic* or *terror*.

In attitudinal healing philosophy, we speak of fear as a state of mind in which we have the sense that we are disconnected from others and from our Divine source. In such moments, as you may confirm, we often feel as though we are in a cocoon of sorts. The world seems to be going on around us, but we are not part of it. Frequently we have difficulty looking others in the eyes or interacting as we might otherwise do. During times of fearfulness, we often feel abandoned by God or detached from our faith. Sometimes we bury ourselves in work, food, shopping, alcohol, or drugs just to dull the feelings of aloneness and insecurity.

If disconnection is the cause of fearful states, *then connection* is the antidote. Since God energy can be equated with love energy, it is important to reconnect in a loving, happy, or fun atmosphere with people who can provide one of these qualities, or to use one of the previously described mental techniques to open the gate to the God-Mind. When we reconnect with our Divine Source, we can discover a miraculous wellspring of protection and grace, which lifts our minds out of darkness into hope, optimism, and clear direction. When we join with others who are encouraging, understanding, or kind, our natural wisdom and buoyancy are reawakened. If these kinds of people are lacking in our lives, we can seek them out in support groups, in therapy, in church, mosque, or synagogue, or the like. Sometimes we have to literally push ourselves out the door, or ask for help when it's uncomfortable to do so, but remember that people are loving by nature, and there are those that are ready, willing, and eager to help when needed.

Sometimes when fear threatens to overwhelm us, we can become spiritual warriors, standing up to it, telling it that we are not going to put up with it, and that fear or no fear, we are going to live our lives fully and satisfyingly! On occasion, I have spoken assertively and sternly to my fear by making a statement such as, "Ok, fear, I see you, and I accept you, but you will not rule my life! I have many things I want to do and I am doing them! So, if you insist of being here, you will sit on a chair in the corner while I go about my other business!" Oddly enough, when I do this, my fear dissipates, and I am freed to move on and even enjoy my activities.

When we're afraid, we often feel shaky or anxious and we may seek out nerve calming drugs. Frequently, this is appropriate when prescribed by an educated doctor, and it can greatly aid the growth process. However, many of these drugs can be addictive and should be used with caution for a temporary time period in conjunction with the help of a trained psychotherapist, clergyman, or counseling professional.

In the best of all circumstances, fear can be used as a catalyst for personal development. It is what is often experienced when we have dropped into a "gully" in our evolutionary process, and its purpose is to prompt us to reach for new learning, new ways of establishing peace and opening our hearts to love. If we allow ourselves to accept, acknowledge and express our fears in a safe place, while using all of the spiritual/mental tools available to us, we can catapult ourselves forward in an amazing way. Fear can be the greatest of gifts to us, in that it pushes us to grow toward love, wisdom, and faith.

ANGER

In our world, one of the most widespread beliefs is that others are to blame for our woes. We expend enormous energy attacking others physically, verbally, or silently with the erroneous perception that this somehow makes us powerful and therefore safe. When we close our hearts to love, we harden toward each other and forget that we are all connected—joined by our earthly existence and by an all-pervasive God-Force.

Anger is a universal human emotion, which can be quite difficult to uproot because of the feigned strength it provides us to conceal hurt or woundedness, which so often lies beneath. To allow ourselves to feel hurt is to put ourselves in a position of weakness, vulnerability, and fragility, whereas to rage at someone gives us the make-believe notion that we are powerful and secure. Anger may even feel good temporarily as we spew out the energetic contents of long-held resentments and irritations.

However, the truth is that anger ultimately hurts us, for what we put out into the Universe can only come back to us. The Buddha told us, "Holding onto anger is like grasping a hot coal with the intent of throwing it at someone else; but you are the one who gets burned."

Therefore, when we decide to let go of our anger, we do it not for another person, but for ourselves. If it benefits someone else, it is an additional bonus, but if we offer ourselves this gift, we liberate ourselves from a good deal of suffering, and we move ourselves into a place of greater compassion and inner peace.

When dealing with anger, it is important to understand that true power comes only from our ability to tune in to, connect with, and reap the benefits of the Divine Spirit, which supports and oversees our well-being through its supreme love. Anger can be dissipated and replaced with compassion by using what we have learned to open our minds to the flow of superconscious material. Only when we do this, can we feel truly masterful and powerful, for we have then created our own peace of mind and are now in a position to offer this to others.

With that said, I realize that it is not always easy to free ourselves from an angry state of mind. Sometimes we are stuck and can't see clearly enough to choose another road. I remember years ago driving to my hometown, which was about four hours away. I was angry at the world and some "significant others" at the time, and was stewing about it when I heard a "pop" behind me. Suddenly my car began to swerve and as I somehow pulled myself to the side of the expressway, I discovered that I had a flat tire, which made me even angrier. After an interminable amount of time waiting for service, the tire was finally replaced with a spare so that I could move on. With my anger intact, I made it to my hometown, only to find, the next morning, that I had another flat tire on the other side of the car. Exasperated, I had the car towed to a dealership where I had both tires fixed. When I headed home after a couple of days, I was still irritated. I made it almost all the way back when one of the tires decided to flatten again. Well, that was more than I felt I could take, which turned out to be an advantage because it finally sent me to my knees in prayer. I didn't know what else to do. In the inner harbor of my God-Mind, I was told that I must give up my anger in order to experience any kind of comfort. In that miraculous moment, I was able to make the choice to see everything and everyone differently, through the eyes of compassion and love.

As is demonstrated in this story, my anger caused me great anguish, so who was I hurting? Only myself. That was the Universe's way of bringing me back to truth. It painted a very clear picture of the damage that anger perpetrates, and the absurdity of holding onto it. Remember that acceptance, acknowledgment, expression in a safe place, and loving support are prime ingredients for the dissipation of anger. It is not wrong to have anger. It is a human emotion common to all of us. However, we do not need to remain stuck in it for long periods of time. The question is not whether we feel anger, but how we respond to it when we feel it.

And finally, when we find ourselves in a state of anger, we can redirect its forceful energy to a positive end by using it to conquer other strong emotions. This allows us to move ourselves forward in some constructive way. That is what is known as being a spiritual warrior. We can all use our powerful anger energy in this way, and therefore reap its benefits rather than its wrath.

WORRY

Worry is the antithesis of present momenting, in that our minds have moved into the future, which is the seat of fear. It is the mind preparing itself for trouble, which has not yet occurred. As Winston Churchill put it, "When I look back on all these worries, I remember the story of the old man who said on his deathbed that he had a lot of troubles in his life, most of which had never happened." So we spend our time thinking about what might come about in the future, therefore creating unnecessary distress in the now.

Worry is the subconscious mind running rampant. Because our past emotionally charged experiences are stored in the subconscious, our conscious mind is constantly being bombarded with its contents, as you may remember from chapter 7. When we are not alert to this, our belief system maintains that our future will look and feel just like our past. That is to say, when some present time situation triggers memories from the past, we mistakenly believe that we will be victims of future circumstances, just as we were in the past, and that there is nothing we can do to alter the course of events.

If, however, we are aware and vigilant, we can see the folly of these habitual beliefs. Since we have been given free choice, we can choose to draw our minds back to the present moment life experience instead of living some dreaded event in the future. As Maya Angelou so beautifully expresses, "We spend precious hours worrying. It would be wise to use that time adoring our families, cherishing our friends, and living our lives." In doing so, we feed ourselves a healthy and delicious helping of comfort and joy.

Like other fear-based emotions, sometimes this is more easily said than done. Bringing our minds back into the present takes practice and, when we are highly fearful about something, our thoughts keep moving into the future in an effort to "fix" or "heal" the emotional turmoil. What we need to realize is that worrying never fixed anything. To the contrary, the continuing practice of being mindful of our present moment experience, allowing ourselves to express our fears with solid support and nonjudgment, and following our inner guidance, can do much to glide us smoothly through a worrisome situation. In this way, we create a new future with new possibilities, based upon present moment choices.

ANXIETY

Anxiety is a form of fear that is frequently subtle, and can often be physically felt (at its extreme) in the form of a rapidly beating heart, sweaty palms, feeling flushed, or (in a milder form) of just being on edge or having the feeling that we are "jumping out of our skin." When we're anxious, the cause of our anxiety is frequently hidden from view. We feel jumpy, irritable, or out of sorts for no known reason, and may remain that way on and off until we examine our thinking and find the cause. Once we know what to work with, we may still experience fear, but we have increased our chances of resolving the situation. Anxiety, like worry, is fear of future happenings, based upon old, mistaken beliefs, and can be handled, once again, by using our mental/spiritual tools, finding loving support and working at shifting our erroneous perceptions.

It has been noted that Western societal consciousness, in particular, has high expectations of its inhabitants. In suburbia, we may be judged harshly if we do not make a significant amount of money, or if we do not complete high school, college, and often beyond. Children are expected to own all the latest toys and gadgets, and to participate in several extra-curricular activities per week. Women are expected to look thin and beautiful, dress well, raise children and simultaneously work, and men are required to bring home a healthy paycheck, although their company is downsizing or cutting back on salaries. Inner-city kids are expected to stay out of trouble, even though there may be danger brewing around every corner, and to do all their school work although they have an after-school job. School systems are expected to educate their students, even though many schools are closing for lack of money. The list goes on and on, and, when we fall short, we can expect severe criticism, even if that criticism lives only in our minds. On top of this, we live in frail human bodies that become ill and eventually die. We are always living with this sense of doom, which can flavor our day-to-day experience. It's no wonder that many of us experience anxiety about the future.

All of this, of course, gives us the opportunity to search for new, more satisfying truths. It gives us the chance to reach deep within, to take classes, to read, to reeducate ourselves in a real spiritual sense. God's truth is not comprised of expectations. It is comprised of love, and the intelligence of the Universe is such that we are each here in the perfect body, experiencing the perfect set of circumstances, for our perfectly unique learning. When we discover that our worth is a given, that we spring from and reside in Divine Spirit, we can allow ourselves to be exactly where we are, doing exactly what we do, in exactly the appropriate fashion for our highest learning and for the highest learning of those around us. When we understand that we are all connected and that we each have our human flaws as well as loving hearts, we can join again with humanity. When we realize that God's job is to craft a safe, peaceful inner environment for us, and that we can call upon God's power and presence to do this, then we needn't be anxious anymore. It is these shifts in perception, which can ultimately dissolve our long-held anxieties.

JEALOUSY

Jealousy is the mistaken perception that others are better than us, or have something we want. It is spawned from self-doubt and a cultural consciousness, again, which praises certain traits and behaviors and condemns others. When we feel jealous, it is a sign that our mind is caught up in comparison, which separates us from others, rather than joins us, in love. To be envious of someone else is to be resistant to our own life, which defies the wisdom of Infinite Intelligence. To accept what is, is to let go of jealousy, comparison, isolation, and separation. Acceptance then leads us into a state of peace, which is what we're each looking for.

Growing up, I was jealous of my older sister's academic abilities, my father's intelligence and strength, my best friend's popularity, and another friend's ease with life. When I became older, I envied my colleague's speaking ability and countless authors and teachers who accomplished more than I did. As I worked on my spiritual reeducation, I came to understand that I didn't have to be everything and I certainly didn't need to be any more than I already was. I could just be myself and trust that this was what I was meant to be and meant to experience in this body in this lifetime. As I accepted myself more and more, I came to honor and appreciate the great diversity within the human race and I could observe the healthy interdependency of mankind in a new way. I was able to see that we are each part of the fabric of what makes this world tick and that we each provide for another the precise personality ingredients that are needed for theirs and our highest learning.

As we learn to love and accept ourselves fully, for each strength, and in spite of each weakness, and as we find purpose and meaning in our life circumstances, we can begin to value the differences we see in others and realize how we each give something to each other and receive something from each other. This will be further discussed in chapter 15.

I have found that one of the most practical ways of dealing with jealousy is to do the following:

> *Sit in silence for five to ten minutes per day or every other day and think about each person you envy, whether you know them personally or not. Ask yourself what they have that you want. Ask yourself what life challenges they might face that you do not. Ask yourself if you have anything in common with them. If you came together in the afterlife, what might they say to you? And you to them? Have a conversation. Now say the words, "jealousy," "cancel," "comparison," "cancel," "envy," "cancel," Now declare, "Our lives are created in such a way that we each think, breathe, behave, accomplish, and look exactly as we're meant to for our supreme good. I trust Infinite Wisdom to guide each of us perfectly toward a loving and peaceful existence!"*

LONELINESS

Loneliness is a state of mind in which we again feel the isolation that fear generates. As we've discussed, when we're afraid, we feel disconnected from others, and that separation causes loneliness. Many of my clients and students over the years have been profoundly lonely. Most have told me that they're hesitant to go out and meet people for fear of rejection. They are people who have been hurt in the past and believe that they will also be hurt in the future. Some are afraid that they're just unlikable and doomed to a life of being alone while certain ones wait for others to show interest in them, and when they don't, it proves that they're no good.

Loneliness is the mistaken perception that one is disconnected from humanity and from God, a belief that is entirely false. When we are lonely, we are unable to see that we are all joined by our commonalities. Our spiritual nature, our minds, our emotions, our physical bodies, which are part of this material world, the air we breathe, the land on which we walk—these are all shared. We each have earthly challenges, we each long for peace, we are each wounded, and there is someone somewhere who shares our interests, our desires, and our values.

Letting go of loneliness requires that *do* something to reconnect with God, or with other people. It requires that we agree to take some risks by moving out into the world where there are people just waiting to open their arms to us. If we're frightened, we can begin with the safest places, perhaps church or temple groups, classes at community centers, going back to school, working with a psychotherapist, calling an old friend and making plans, cuddling with an animal, volunteering where help is needed, etc. The fact is, people need people, and living beings thrive on interaction with other living beings. There is no one in this world undeserving of having relationships. We just need to put the time and energy into creating them. Remember, the past is over. We can create a new future by what we choose to do today!

DEPRESSION/HOPELESSNESS

I experienced depression early on in childhood, for I was a sensitive soul, and earthly life seemed so harsh to me. This depression repeatedly kept cropping up as I grew into adolescence. Much of the time I couldn't put my finger on it, but I just knew something wasn't right with my bickering, demanding family, with angry schoolmates, and of course, with conflict all over the world. I was never comfortable with discord, and frequently removed myself from situations over which I had no control. I would often withdraw into a shell, feeling hopeless, helpless, and frustrated. I felt there was no one to listen to me, no one who understood my point of view, and no one to love me for who I was.

It was Mother Teresa who remarked, "We can cure physical diseases with medicine, but the only cure for loneliness, despair, and hopelessness is love. There are many in the world who are dying for a piece of bread, but there are many more dying for a little love." As I've grown older, I've encountered hundreds of people who have struggled with depression, for as Mother Teresa says, what's lacking in our world is enough love.

When we are babies, we cry when we are uncomfortable. As young children, we cry and carry on when something seems unfair or when we want something that we can't have. If we cry too much or too long without a loving response, we stop crying and stuff our hurt inside. This hurt plagues us through life, in the form of a closed heart that has forgotten joy.

As adolescents, we adopt a point of view, which we want to share with someone else who will respect our thoughts and our position. As we become young adults, we hope that our parents and teachers will support, or at least honor, our career choices. However, too often, people refuse to listen, especially when they disagree with us. When we are invalidated over and over again, we can give up on people, give up on life. Our self-esteem suffers, and it seems like there's no place in this world for us to be safe.

There is also situational depression, such as after the loss of a loved one, during hardship caused by poverty, after a job rejection or layoff, after the birth of a developmentally disabled child, etc. No matter what the cause, loving help is needed to find our way through the darkness. When difficult situations such as these arise, our first response is generally sadness. Sometimes that sadness is unexpressed or unacknowledged because the expectation is that it will not be heard. Sometimes, even when there is listening, it is not of a purely loving and accepting nature. When sadness is not thoroughly understood and embraced, it can turn into depression.

Depression, to me, is a disease of the heart that has closed in response to an unloving environment. Normally, when emotions are expressed and acknowledged in a nurturing atmosphere, they pass through us, allowing us eventually to return to our natural loving self. When this expression is blocked, we suffer and we disconnect from people and from God. We often feel abandoned, alone, unmotivated, and lost. For some, the depression is so deep that hopelessness sets in, and it can take several years of therapy to unravel the string of events that caused such hurt.

However, with the help of a trained psychotherapist, clergy person, or guide who can unconditionally encourage and allow our flow of feelings, depression can lift and joy can reenter. In my experience, love is the most powerful healing force there is. So, as hard as it may seem, when we're depressed, we must seek out people who are nurturing and who are willing and able to walk us through the shadows. This reconnects us to others and brings us back to our wholeness.

If medicine is necessary, keep in mind that it may help us elevate our level of functioning so that we can do the healing work required of us. One important factor to keep in mind is that if anti-depressants are used, they must be allowed three to four weeks to bring about the desired effect. I've worked with several clients who gave them up after a week or two when they felt no different. Sometimes, too, we must try a few different anti-depressants until we find the correct one for us. It is imperative to work with a physician who knows his/her pharmacology and can help us to experiment until we succeed. The key is to take them consistently, according to the doctor's prescription, and to give them a long enough chance to work.

In addition to this, I have learned that one excellent antidote to depression is service. When we are depressed and withdrawn, we have stopped giving of ourselves to others, and so the positive flow that is produced from such giving has been cut off. Thus, we are not able to receive the good feeling that comes from offering help. Remember, depression is a form of fear, and extending love in any way is fear's opposite, contradicting the separation we feel when depressed. Giving of ourselves with love creates joining, connection, and peace of mind. It may not be an easy choice to make at the time, but it is always available to us as an avenue out of darkness.

Finally, our psycho-spiritual tools discussed in chapters 8 and 9 are of immense value, each one bringing its own gift. This is a time to develop our faith, to practice prayer and surrender. Spiritual reading can be inspirational, motivational, and soothing, while affirmation can strengthen our minds. Above all, acceptance of our feelings and self-forgiveness can go a long way toward healing our hurts and creating long-forgotten happiness.

SADNESS/GRIEF

Life is full of letting go. We're born; we die. Those we love die. The Buddha said that impermanence is the law in our world and that the only thing we can be sure of is change. Jobs end, divorce happens, homes burn down, friends move away, pets are euthanized, etc. It sometimes seems that we must say good-bye before we are emotionally prepared. And even when we seem to have gotten ready, loss can feel troubling and sometimes excruciating. Sadness and grief are part of living. As evolving creatures, we must let go in order to bring in the new. When the Universe has decided that it is time for a new learning, it arranges for space to be made to accommodate the additional knowledge. Unfortunately, these new learnings are not always on our agenda—only God's. Thus the loss can be difficult to accept. This is why we often experience shock, deep grief, and even anger when faced with loss.

Like depression, we must seek out nurturing places to express our feelings, whether it be with a mental health professional, a minister or rabbi, in a support group, or with a trusted friend. Again, connection is important here. Otherwise, we can end up in deep depression or hopelessness. There are many books that have been written by authors who have experienced their own bereavements. These can be a source of comfort and provide someone else with whom to identify. A woman I know who lost her husband after many years of marriage. She reread a writer's story numerous times during the course of the first year. She said it got her through one of the most challenging times of her life.

Tears are meant to be shed. Crying is the body's way of dealing with the pain of loss and of making space for the new. Sometimes others become uncomfortable with our sadness and imply that we should be done already. Sometimes they tell us so, and sometimes they withdraw from us. This is a sign of their discomfort, not of anything that we're doing wrong. It's okay to cry, to rant and rave, and to talk about our loss over and over again until it passes through us. Eventually, if we allow ourselves this freedom of expression, especially in a loving and safe environment, we will move on, a little wiser and a bit more compassionate than we were before this all happened.

It's important during a time of loss to stay as much as possible in the present moment and to take one day at a time. It is impossible to understand exactly how life will look once we get through the grief. It must unfold, and it is best not to worry excessively about the future. With time, everything in our lives will shift about. New relationships will form, old relationships may become closer, and newfound activities will capture our interest. This is the Divine Spirit's way of taking care of us through its unconditional love.

The most favorable way to move through situations of grief and loss is to trust in the supreme intelligence of the God-Force and to surrender our well-being into its arms. When we are able to do this, we will receive all of the support and resources that we need to move through this time period with grace and greater ease.

DISAPPOINTMENT/FRUSTRATION

When I was in college, I rushed a sorority my freshman year. At the time, sororities and fraternities were popular, and since I was at a large University where one could feel lost at times, I viewed sorority life as the place to be. I wanted it more than anything, and maybe for that reason went into rush a bit nervous. I was drawn to the girls in a couple of houses and I really wanted them to like me and choose me as one of their sisters. I wanted it so badly that when I was denied membership, I was devastated. Disappointment and frustration flooded in, and I was upset for an entire semester. Had I known what I know now about surrendering to the will of a Higher Intelligence, I might have been able to handle the situation better. I might have felt my disappointment, but it would have passed through me more quickly.

We all have times of disappointment in our lives and when we work hard at something with a particular goal in mind, if we don't fulfill our objective, we can become quite frustrated. The Buddha taught us that one of the great causes of suffering is desire, and if we could just allow every experience to unfold as it must, without judging it, we would be far happier. However, most of us move through life with our own agendas, which we often make mandatory in our minds. We desire and even expect many things per week, and if we are unaware, we can create inner havoc. "I want that promotion. If I don't get it, then something's wrong with me." I want an A in that class. If I don't get it, then I'm stupid." "Bill should pick up his clothes. I've asked him over and over. If he doesn't, then he's a creep!" "Mary should call me this week. If she doesn't, then she must not like me." "I want Jason to ask me to the dance. If that doesn't happen, I'll be devastated." As we can see, we often decide that if we don't get what we want, then ours, or someone else's, worth is at stake.

I have found that the antidote to disappointment and frustration is the practice of acceptance and surrender. It's remembering that the events of our lives are more than we might be able to understand at this point in time. It's recalling that Divine Wisdom is in charge and is always helping us become less afraid, less angry, and less stressed through its absolute love for us. If we resist what is happening in our lives, we invite disappointment and frustration. If we can practice acceptance and surrender, these feelings may be with us for a short time but will dissolve more rapidly. If we can work on loving and accepting ourselves no matter what happens, then our faith in the Universe will grow as we come to understand the lessons we are learning and as we eventually feel enfolded in the peace of God.

In conclusion, all human beings have fears, and fear is found in every emotional state. Learning to cope with our feelings in an improved manner requires practice of simple principles. The following steps can be helpful for bringing about greater harmony within. They needn't be done in the order shown, but these are good guidelines with which to begin your practice.

1. Accept your situation.
2. Surrender your emotions to a higher power.
3. Get support.
4. Express your feelings in a safe place.
5. Focus on your present-moment experience.
6. Affirm positive statements.
7. Let time pass.

LEARNING THROUGH EXPERIENCE

A. *Consider these questions or activities:*

1. *What emotions are most difficult for you?*
2. *What might you practice to handle them better?*
3. *Write these emotions on the left-hand side of a piece of paper. On the right-hand side, list words or phrases which might help you to cope in an improved way. Refer to this list whenever you are troubled in any way.*

B. *Affirmations for coping with strong emotions:*

Feel free to change the wording in any way.

(Fear) The love of the God Power within me is stronger than any fear that arises!
(Fear) I can handle anything that happens in my life!

(Anger) I see only the good in ______________!
(Anger) I live my life through the eyes of love and forgiveness!

(Worry) I live in the now and I can handle what is happening in the present moment!
(Worry) Divine Spirit always gives me the strength to cope with anything that may happen anytime!

(Anxiety) I see the cause of this anxiety, and I am wise enough and strong enough to deal with it!
(Anxiety) (Use "fear" affirmations)

(Jealousy) I compare myself to no one. I am perfectly wonderful just the way I am!

(Jealousy) I have everything I need to live fully and peacefully!

(Loneliness) I move out into the world easily and have several fantastic people to connect with!

(Loneliness) I see myself surrounded by people (and animals)!

(Depression) I am free to be me and am respected and heard by others!

(Depression/Hopelessness) I am happy, fulfilled, motivated, and productive. I love life!

(Grief/Sadness)) I move through my grief easily and receive all the support I need!

(Grief/Sadness) I take life one day at a time and know that happiness is inside of me just waiting to blossom again!

(Disappointment/Frustration) I accept this situation completely, knowing God is with me!

(Disappointment/Frustration) I surrender my life to God's will and know that I am led to comfort and joy!

If thou art pained by an external thing,
it is not this thing that disturbs thee,
but thy own judgment about it.
And it is in thy power
to wipe out this judgment now.
—Marcus Aurelius

CHAPTER 14

Health and Illness

AS mentioned earlier, twenty-five years ago when my first-born child was two years old, I collapsed from fatigue and nervousness. I had been in school working on my master's degree in guidance and counseling, while, at the same time, I was experiencing the wonders, trials, and tribulations of being a new mother. While many mothers are capable of handling that amount of stress, for some reason, I was not, and my exhausted body broke down, sending me into a cycle of fear that is unforgettable. How would I care for this child? How would I finish my degree? What would everyone think? How weak I would look! Maybe I was dying!

Although I searched medical avenues for answers, most doctors could find no answers for me, and eventually diagnosed me with chronic fatigue syndrome, which has, in various forms, been my companion for significant periods of time since then. The syndrome, characterized by fatigue, gastrointestinal pain and distress, and muscle/joint soreness and stiffness, has waxed and waned over time. It has brought frustration and disappointment at times, and yet, more important, it has moved me steadily into miraculous, wondrous places of greater wisdom and increased levels of mastery over hardship. The illness has granted me the ability to see life from a brand-new perspective, and to feel a connectedness I had never before experienced. It has propelled me into a spiritual haven of sorts, and thrust me toward the goal that I, consciously or unconsciously, have invariably pursued, that of inner peace.

We live in a society in which illness is almost always perceived as an enemy. For most people, sickness is something to get rid of as quickly as possible. It is a bother, a nuisance, an irritation, a pest, or an aggravation. Yet, illness consistently exists in our world. Doctors' offices are overflowing with individuals complaining of everything from coughs and colds to the agonizing pain of life-threatening disease. It seems that just as we find a cure for one disease, another crops up to confound us again. According to Kat Duff, author and counselor, "Illness is a thread, like in weaving, that runs through our entire lives. It is a central component of human experience."

When people are sick, understandably, they want to feel better as quickly as possible. Sickness is fraught with physical and emotional pain and discomfort, and it is seen as an unwanted intruder, often arriving at the worst time possible. Therefore, we, as a society, generally focus on curing physical symptoms, while mental, spiritual, and psychological growth, are often ignored. Many of us were raised in families where the belief was, "If you have your health, you have everything!" We grew up deeming physical health the "God" of happiness, strength, and comfort, rather than focusing on the attainment of a healthy mind and spirit—one capable of creating a high quality, fulfilling, and well-functioning life, no matter what the circumstances of the body are. It's not that it isn't easier to function more fully and happily when the body is in a healthy "physical" state, but too often, present-day consciousness is concentrated on only the reduction of physical symptoms, with disregard to the amazingly potent mental, spiritual, and emotional qualities of our human makeup. Frequently, people who are physically ill lose hope that they can lead full, meaningful lives, when it is most always possible in some way.

If we move beyond the physical, we discover a mental/spiritual/energetic world, which can ultimately lead to self-awareness, meaning, greater empowerment and peace of mind. Medicine is beginning to change, as we bring more complementary and alternative treatments into medical practice. Medical schools are starting to offer electives that are more holistic in nature. Some doctors have written books about mind-body medicine and the power of thoughts to heal us either on an emotional level or a physical level; and there are numerous accounts of patients' healing journeys during long, arduous illnesses. These stories refer not only to the physical treatments, which patients have discovered, but to what these individuals have learned about themselves, about life, and about love, during the course of sickness.

In this chapter, we will examine some of the novel ways to view health challenges and various mental and spiritual coping techniques that can lead to physical healing, diminished symptoms, and/or emotional well-being.

HEALTH: A STATE OF MIND

According to attitudinal healing philosophy, "health" cannot be simply defined as health of the physical body, for even if we possess abundant physical health, we may be depressed, anxious, angry, or afraid. And vice versa, sometimes those of us who are physically ill may be living wonderful lives, full of quality, fulfillment, and meaning. Regardless of the physical health of the body, the opportunity to live happily and to live well is always present. That is why, in Attitudinal Healing, we speak of "health" as "health of the mind," not the physical body. Simply put, I've learned to see health as a state of being or a state of mind, rather than a state of physical comfort or wellness.

Susan Trout, PhD, author, professor, researcher, and psycho-neurologist, defines health as, "a state of mind that is harmonious, active, flexible, alive, and energized." It has nothing to do with the state of the body. In basic terms, health is a state of inner peace. Attitudinal Healing proponents as well as many forward-thinking psychotherapists and doctors now challenge the notion that we are victims of external circumstances, such as short-term, chronic, or even life-threatening illness. We are now beginning to understand that we have the power to create our emotional reality through the thoughts we choose to place in our minds, by releasing our fears in a safe environment, and by forming new perceptions, which are based upon love, acceptance, compassion, and truth.

Susan Trout, in her book *To See Differently,* gives a wonderful example of handling illness this way. The story is poignant and worth repeating here:

> *While working on this chapter, I [Susan] was preparing for a second pilgrimage to Medjugorje, the village in Yugoslavia where an apparition of the Virgin Mary has been occurring since 1981. Our lady has appeared throughout history and has been a messenger and guide in times of great conflict. Physical and spiritual healings are associated with her appearances.*
>
> *Fra Jozo, former parish priest in Medjugorje, tells the story of two Italian women, both confined to wheelchairs, who came to Medjugorje in hopes of physical healing. The elder of the two women was healed. The younger, Manuela, remained in her wheelchair. The one who was healed returned home, delighted at being able to walk again; Manuela stayed behind to give thanks and praise to God. They both came with the desire to be healed, and they were both healed. But healing is not only physical; it is something that takes place in the heart. Manuela was healed in the heart. Full of joy, she praised God for having come to her, for shedding light on the cross she carried, for showing her its value and meaning. She*

understood that from her wheelchair, she could bring people spiritual solace, telling them about the love of God, about goodness, about the wisdom that patience can bring. Manuela took far greater joy home in her heart than the woman who went home able to walk. The church was grateful for both blessings. Deeply grateful.

In telling this story, Fra Jozo shares his conviction that true healing is an inner one. Our Lady's message in Medjugorje is peace, that peace which begins in the heart and extends outward. Since health is inner peace, healing begins within.

ILLNESS AS A PURPOSEFUL OCCURRENCE

Through the years, as I've had to cope with chronic fatigue syndrome, I've experienced a shift in my view of illness. I now see all physical and mental illness as an opportunity to heal the mind of its fears and therefore, as an opportunity for spiritual growth. Illness has the "forcefulness" to propel us forward and upward in our evolutionary journey by surfacing and displaying our inner conflicts. It is a forceful catalyst because it can be uncomfortable, undesirable, or painful and it is this very discomfort that causes us to seek relief.

According to author and minister, Bob Trowbridge, "Illness is not an evil, but is simply a bearer of messages of information about what's going on in your head. Don't shoot the messenger." What Reverend Trowbridge is saying is that when we resist illness, we lose the opportunity to find meaning and use it in a beneficial way. The purpose of sickness may open wonderful new doors, even though it may close others. What is good for the soul is infinitely different from the world of the body. What seems good or pleasurable from a purely physical perspective, may indeed be harmful and useless from a soul perspective. From a metaphysical point of view, the soul is unfolding and evolving toward a state of purity, love, or God-centeredness, and may require bodily distress to further its goals.

If viewed in a different manner, sickness can be the vehicle through which we see the areas of our lives that need modification. For example, perhaps our lifestyle is out of balance, as we find ourselves running from here to there, never taking a moment to catch our breath. Maybe we are eating too many fattening, nutrition-less foods, or forgetting to eat because we're so busy. Perhaps a relationship needs to be healed or released, or we have been wanting to look for a new job but just haven't. Possibly we feel trapped at work and can't figure a way to get out. Maybe we have been reckless with our money and illness is forcing us to reevaluate what is most important in our life and find new ways of being materially secure.

Whatever the problem, illness can be a signal that change is required. It can demand that we look inside to see what isn't working and search for new answers. It can push us to explore our spiritual life, which may have long been ignored. Or it can impel us to learn more lessons from the Universe about developing the attributes we discussed in chapter 3, such as faith, courage, forgiveness, surrender, hope, and the like. Illness, then, can be seen as a gift instead of a wicked, offensive, or undesirable intruder. As illness takes on meaning, some of its associated awfulness tends to dissipate, and exciting new soul growth starts to occur.

Kat Duff is a psychotherapist and author who struggled with her own illness. Her sense of need, at the time, prompted her research into the ancient science of alchemy in an attempt to better understand the processes involved in disease. In her book *The Alchemy of Illness* Duff recounts her findings, which I found to be quite fascinating. I relate her ideas here:

> Alchemy, according to the World Book Encyclopedia, was a combination of medieval chemistry, magic and mysticism, which attempted to change a baser metal into silver or gold. Many alchemists also

tried to find a magic cure-all to lengthen life and find eternal youth. Although they failed, and some alchemists were seen as foolish, their research helped the science of chemistry to evolve.

Originally, the alchemists' attempts to make gold or silver commenced by using the rawest, most unsightly metal that could be found: lead. Because alchemy concerns itself with the power of transformation, this would mean, symbolically and psychologically, that spiritual healing must begin with the issues within us that make us feel most despicable, humiliated or afraid. What better place to look, then, but to disease to lead us to a place of spiritual growth and healing? For in illness, we are constantly confronted with the parts of ourselves which are most disliked—our shames and indignities, as well as our greatest fears, frustrations and angers.

During illness there is a drawing inward-making the exit from the outer world into an inner world. At first we feel as though we have no control. But this can teach us how to surrender, since there is no other choice. We can be pushed beyond the point of grasping or caring—beyond our attachment to anything worldly. Rigidity leaves, and greater flexibility is produced. We must open to a bigger view, a larger picture. We're pushed to commune with another part of our mind, the Cosmic, Divine, all-intelligent part of our mind, which can be such a magnificent teacher, showing us where we have erred in our thinking and how and where we may improve our lives. These are moments when we can feel the peace of God, which underlies all of the outer turmoil. To discover this can be a great revelation.

Thus, this alchemical view presents what is endeavoring to happen, spiritually and psychologically, through the process of illness. Duff states, "I've heard it said that illness is an attempt to escape the truth. I suspect it's an attempt to embody the whole truth."

With that in mind, it is clear that considering sickness from the perspective of the alchemist produces a much more positive view of a human experience which has traditionally been met with judgment, resistance, and fear. In this vein, illness is not seen as a failure. Rather, it is a crucial gateway to another world—to another way of thinking, living, and being.

COPING WITH ILLNESS

In the previous sections, we discussed the ideas that health can be redefined as a "peaceful state of mind," and that illness can be seen as a purposeful occurrence. However, even with that knowledge, it is hard to deny that dealing with disease can be quite difficult. Physical symptoms do make us uncomfortable, and sometimes either the physical or emotional pain involved can feel unbearable. The good news is that our tools from chapters 8 and 9 still apply. We are beginning to have a repertoire on which to fall back. As we develop these skills, we are more apt to move through illness with greater ease.

There are several prominent authors who have focused on improving the way we handle and relate to disease. Bernie Siegel, MD is a doctor who has dedicated his life to teaching the medical profession about the mind-body connection in healing. He has worked with cancer patients, providing an innovative format for patient empowerment and participation in their own healing processes, through many varied personal growth techniques. Jon Kabat-Zinn is the director of the Stress Reduction Center at the University of Massachusetts Medical Center. Kabat-Zinn, working with ill people of all types, teaches his patients mindfulness meditation, allowing them to be exactly where they are without judging their experience. He teaches self-awareness and sees healing as a metamorphosis or an alteration of attitude with the accompanying positive emotional state of being. Linda Noble Topf, a strong supporter of Attitudinal Healing, and an MS patient herself, promotes the idea that the ill person is not a label or a "set of symptoms in a medical book," and she vigorously believes in the power to choose peace-producing thoughts. She suggests that as the ill person becomes more self-aware through observation of thought patterns, reeducation, and consciousness-raising exercises, he or she is more able to change his thoughts from those that are disturbing to those that are more comfortable and peaceful.

My intent here is to present several guidelines common to these authors' belief systems, which can help us to move more steadily and calmly through illness. Specific coping exercises will be given at the end of the chapter. Hopefully, if you are dealing with sickness of any kind, you will engage in these exercises in the attempt to know yourselves better and accept all that you are. They can also produce great comfort during periods of distress and be quite effective if given effort, energy and time.

The guidelines to which I have referred, for coping with illness, are the following:

1. Allow yourself to experience, without judgment, all the feelings that move through you, and remember that if you can **accept** these, they will pass away more quickly. Let yourself be sad, angry, frustrated, etc. with empathy for yourself. You are not alone. Others would feel the same way.

2. Let go of trying to control your present situation and face what's happening to you, while surrendering yourself to Divine Love. **Trust** that your highest good is being done, and that this illness will eventually provide you with greater inner strength.

3. See illness as an impetus for psycho-spiritual growth and self-awareness—an **opportunity** to learn lessons.

4. View sickness as a **redirection** in your life and as moving you toward being your authentic, best self.

5. Be **compassionate** toward every part of you, even the parts of you that you have not forgiven. As you become more compassionate for yourself, you will be able to extend yourself with **kindness** to others. This is more fulfilling than anything else for your soul.

6. Remember that treating yourself with compassion, **love**, **forgiveness**, **empathy**, and **nonjudgment** will stimulate your immune system and possibly diminish painful symptoms. It may also have a positive effect on your recovery process.

7. Remember to have **patience**. Infinite Intelligence has a plan for you, which will unfold in a precise way at a precise time. You can't rush the process. If you are focused on "getting there," then you can't center your mind on the now.

8. Take some time to put your attention on **giving to others** in some way, even if small. This can bring you out of a suffering stance into a happy one, help you physically, emotionally, and karmically, and create inner peace and great fulfillment.

9. View death or recurrence of disease as further opportunities for growth and evolution. Focus on making the most of the **present moment**, not on being physically well or alive.

If you notice, certain words in the above guidelines have been highlighted so that your memory will be triggered when you are having a difficult time. You may want to write them on a card, which you can carry around with you, or several cards which you place in significant spots around your house. The words listed are:

Accept
Trust
Opportunity
Redirection
Compassion
Kindness

Love
Forgiveness
Empathy
Non-judgment
Patience
Giving to others
Present moment

In moments of suffering during illness, look at this list and note which word has the most meaning for you at this moment. What can you learn from this word? How can you use it right now? You'll find the answers inside you. Remember, the God-Force is directing you if you will only listen.

In conclusion, the challenge of illness is a universal phenomenon. All human beings encounter sickness at one time or another during their lifetime. Illness carries with it emotional and physical discomfort and pain and, therefore, has traditionally been seen through the eyes of negativity. However, I believe that sickness and disease can be seen as a powerful evolutionary force for the journey of the soul. It is often a call to prayer, a reaching out to the Divine in order to bring us into communion with a comforting higher and wiser power. Since Infinite Intelligence provides the perfect circumstances for the spiritual and psychological journey, illness can be seen as a powerful catalyst, which helps to create inner strength, perseverance, compassion, patience, and love. To be healthy is a state of mind, which embraces all aspects of living and all parts of the self. To be healthy is to be at peace.

LEARNING THROUGH EXPERIENCE

A. *Examine the following questions:*

1. *How do you feel about being sick? Has this chapter changed your ideas about illness? About health? If so, how?*
2. *When do you consider yourself healthy? Think of a time when you felt exceptionally healthy. What were the circumstances?*
3. *How do you cope with illness in your life? Are you resistant? Are you accepting of it? Does it scare you? If so, what are you afraid of? How might you better handle illness?*

B. *Affirmations for Coping with Illness:*

1. *I choose to remember that this illness has a purpose in my life, and it is a great teacher to me!*
2. *My body is in perfect balance. The energy flows freely and completely through every part of me!*
3. *Divine Spirit now melts and dispels every negative thought in my mind and every negative condition in my body!*
4. *I am filled with healing light and illuminating wisdom. I am completely healthy!*
5. *I totally accept myself in every way, and I see my worth wherever I go!*
6. *I let go of attacking myself with condemning thoughts and my body responds joyfully!*
7. *I choose inner peace in spite of my illness. I am strong, confident, and happy. I am living life to its fullest!*

C. Prayers and Inspirations:

On Sickness

In sickness I turn to You, O God,
as a child turns to a parent
for comfort and help.
Strengthen within me the
wondrous power of healing
that You have implanted in Your children.
Guide my doctors and nurses
that they may speed my recovery.
Let the knowledge of Your love
comfort my dear ones,
lighten their burdens,
and renew their faith.
May my sickness
not weaken my faith in You,
nor diminish my love
for other human beings.
From my illness my I gain
a truer appreciation of life's gifts,
a deeper awareness of life's blessings,
and a fuller sympathy for all who are in pain.

Jewish prayer from the New
Union Home Prayer Book

On Sickness

My God and God of all generations,
in my great need I pour out my heart to You.

The long days and weeks of suffering
are hard to endure.
In my struggle, I reach out for the help
that only You can give.
Let me feel that You are near,
and that Your care enfolds me.
Rouse in me the strength to
overcome my weakness,
and brighten my spirit
with the assurance of Your love.
Make me grateful for the care and concern
that are expended on my behalf.
Help me to sustain the hopes
of my dear ones, as they strive to
strengthen and encourage me.
May the healing power You have placed within me
give me strength to recover,
so that I may proclaim with all my being:
I shall not die, but live and declare the works of the Lord.

Jewish prayer from the New Union
Home Prayer Book

Prayer for Healing

Dear God,
My body is sick and I am so scared, so weak, so sad,
Please heal me, Lord.
Whatever the words I am supposed to say,
whatever the thoughts that would set me free,
I am willing to have them shine into my mind.
For I wish to be released. Please give me a miracle.

Please give me hope. Please give me peace.
Lift me up beyond the regions of my pain and despair.
Prepare each cell to be born anew into
health and happiness, peace and love.
For You are the power, not this sickness.
You are the truth, not this illusion.
You are my salvation, not the doctor.
I am willing to rise, to let go all false thinking,
to release this false condition.
For this is not freedom, and I wish to be free.
This is not peaceful, and I desire peace.
This is not Your will for me, that I would suffer or feel pain.
I accept Your will for me.
I accept your healing.
I accept your love.
Please, dear God, help me.
Take me home.
AMEN.

—Marianne Williamson, from Illuminata

Healing Thoughts

In this moment, and in all moments that I live in this physical body, I am creating this body by my thoughts and my emotions. To the best of my ability, I now set my intention and my will to create as much love, beauty, and harmony in this day as I can. If I go forth to the best of my ability to do this, then I will assume that the effect that my inner life will have on my body in this day will be very beneficial. I trust this to be true, and I release all fear that it is not.

No harm can come to my being as I am healing myself of this physical and emotional pain. I am eternal, and this challenge is temporary. I will let this emotional pain rise up to be expressed and experienced by me, to be understood, and eventually to be healed. Whatever step of the healing process this moment may be, I live it now, and I rejoice in being alive. I bring as much love and trust to this moment of healing as I possibly can.

—Ron Scolastico

If you were all alone in the Universe
with no one to talk to, no one with which to share
the beauty of the stars, to laugh with, to touch,
what would be your purpose in life?
It is other life, it is love, which gives your life meaning.
This is harmony.
We must discover the joy of each other,
the joy of challenge, the joy of growth.
—Mitsugi Saotome

CHAPTER 15

Relationships

I had a married friend once who remarked that if she and her husband could have houses side by side instead of living in the same space, she would be very happy. Another friend called me every day as she struggled through a nasty divorce. Then there was a client who had an estranged son, and a woman who had felt alienated from her family for many years. It seems no matter whom I've known, each person has had his or her relationship challenges. Like health, one of the larger human concerns, relationships rate high on the list of importance in human affairs.

As we travel through life, we find ourselves constantly in relationships with others. Some relationships we like. Those are the easy ones. But others open us to reservoirs of hurt, fright, pain, or angry indignation. Relationships define society, as people and groups of people find that they must relate to each other in an unending score of interactions. Whether the relationships are country/country, leader/leader, teacher/student, employee/employer, worker/co-worker, husband/wife, partner/partner, parent/child or the like, we find ourselves linked with others, for better or for worse.

Relationships are meant to heal us, to chisel the jewel, which is our core, so to speak. I've heard stories of those who have gone off into the woods in meditative retreat for months at a time. During the time they live in the woods, they are happy, peaceful, even blissful. When they come back into the world and associate with others, as they must, all that bliss immediately drops away, and they are faced with the hardened, closed, secretive parts of themselves, which have not yet been healed. It is as though the person in the woods was only the undisturbed diamond in the rough, waiting to be cut, molded, and fashioned into the exquisite stone that reflected his greatest beauty. For where else can we better learn the lessons of love than in relationships?

In every encounter we have, there is the perfection of Infinite Intelligence working to heal us of our erroneous thinking, working to bring us into alignment with our Divine nature. There are no mistakes. If we find ourselves in relationship with another, then that person is our teacher and we are theirs. In other words, this is the person best suited for our education at that moment.

In harmonious relationships, we receive validation, support, and a healthy respect for who we are. In inharmonious ones, we are learning to accept, to appreciate, to forgive, to honor, to feel compassion, to be patient, to communicate nonviolently, to be honest, etc. Our lessons apply to others and to ourselves. When we have learned what is needed, we move on to other relationships that further Universal teachings. Some relationships are meant to last a lifetime and others a shorter period of time. When there is a balance of learning on both sides, the relationship remains intact. When the balance of learning shifts, the relationship breaks apart.

Each of us sees the world through our own filter, which takes into account our past experiences and programming. Therefore, the way we view ourselves, our world, and each other, are perceptions, not facts. When we change our perception of other people and of ourselves, we can change the way we feel inside. We can learn that we don't have to agree with another person in order to have a healthy, fulfilling relationship. We can learn to honor each point of view and to hold compassion for the wounded part of each of us, which sometimes engages in destructive behavior. As we resolve our own inner conflict, we heal our relationships. Moreover, as we, as a species, learn what it takes to heal relationships, we develop the capacity to heal our world of its wars and turmoil. This is where it all begins—inside of us. Thus, we embark here on a fuller understanding of the finer points involved in healing relationships—from the inside out.

GIVING UP JUDGMENT

As we've discussed previously, we each grew up in fear-based consciousness, the predominant thought system of our world. That often-turbulent belief system is full of judgment and evaluation, which we've been taught since an early age. It's a world of perception in which we pit ourselves against others in a never-ending one up-manship or one down-manship stance. We are either better or worse than someone else—weaker or stronger, prettier or uglier, smarter or dumber. And others are compared to each other in much the same way. John's not as good a speaker as Brian. Helen's more successful than Judy. Joe's more charming than Charles. Irene's got it all together while Walter is falling apart. And on and on it goes. Our physical eyes see the differences among people and our programmed minds compare those dissimilarities. It's true that our personalities are distinct from one another, and our journeys here are entirely diverse, but rating those differences on some imaginary scale, is where we get into trouble and cause ourselves and others suffering.

I'm reminded of the man at the dentist's office whom I saw some time ago, who looked so self-assured, a business executive who, I thought, must growl for a living. He seemed so different from the person I was, not always so confident, but intent on being kind to others. And then I smiled as I realized that he, too, would be as vulnerable as I, sitting in that dentist's chair awaiting the shrill sound of the drill and having to relinquish all control to a man we hardly knew. And I thought to myself, "We're all human. We're all helpless babies at one time. We all eventually leave this Earth, we all sleep at night and have skin, bones, and muscles. In addition, we all need love to thrive." I realized then, that each of us has manifested in the perfect and particular manner needed, in order to learn the specific lessons suitable for this moment of our evolutionary journey. At our root, we are beings of nature, designed by and composed of, the very same Divine energy. No one is better than anyone else. We just are what we are.

Judgment comes from inside of us. If we are judging others, we are merely judging ourselves, for we can only give to others what already exists internally. When we judge another, we have forgotten our own inner goodness. If we are not conscious of our own loving inner core, seeing another's loving center only reminds us that we are lacking in some way. So we judge others to make ourselves feel better.

However, how many of us can be happy judging another? Happiness cannot be found in the harsh world of judgment. Being happy requires the ability to see the loving essence in each person with whom we come into contact, no matter what their outer appearance looks like. In Attitudinal Healing we call this "seeing the light, not the lampshade."

At a conference I attended many years ago, a beautiful and spiritual woman told a story that demonstrates the power of letting go of judgment. She told us that each day when she went to work, she had to take a boat across the water. The cost of the boat ride was seventy-five cents, which she made sure she always had in her pocket. On the other side of the water there sat, day after day, a filthy and unkempt bagman, holding out a tin can for passersby, hoping that someone would be kind that day. Well, this woman never could bring herself to look at the homeless man. The sight of him scared her and the thought of him disgusted her—until one day. She was on her way home from work and was approaching the dock when she reached in her pocket and realized the seventy-five cents she needed was nowhere to be found. As a matter of fact, she had no money on her at all. Because she *had* to get home, with a deep breath and pounding heart, she made her way to the man and asked, "Do you, by any chance, have seventy-five cents? I have no money and need to get home." Well, with no hesitation at all, the bagman replied, "Sure I do! Here!" And he reached in his can, pulling out the three quarters she so badly needed. With that, they both smiled, feeling warmed by the very special encounter that had just taken place. They then struck up a conversation and ultimately became fast friends, opening the doors to the happiness that then became a permanent part of their relationship.

Our judgments about others only cause us harm. It is, of course, quite a task to let go of all our criticisms and adulations. They are a part of us and a part of our upbringing and conditioning, which cannot be erased overnight. However, as we use our previously discussed tools for psycho-spiritual growth, we are continually making progress in this direction. As we can see from the story above, relinquishing judgment can bring inner peace, contentment and joy to all parties involved. For ourselves, it is the tender and warm feeling of having given something through seeing another's true essence. For the recipients of our nonjudgment, it is a release from the bonds that have held them prisoner, the bonds that have tightened and established their belief in their own imperfection. Thus, our effort to see, more clearly, the equality of each human being, is richly rewarded.

ATTACK, BLAME, DEFEND

I remember once many years ago, sitting in a board meeting for a nonprofit organization of which I was a part. We were having a heated discussion, and one of the board members was clearly angry, even enraged, as he proceeded to scream his way through our meeting, verbally mutilating our stunned and silent group. Dark energy reared its ugly head, spraying its poisonous fumes onto a vulnerable, yet good-natured audience. The urge to yell back, to accuse, to defend, became unbearably strong within us, as we attempted to gather ourselves together in order to maintain a sense of calm and peace. I recall thinking to myself that this man was crazy, and, for a short time, I found myself shocked and repulsed by his behavior.

It was some years later that I realized that I, too, had anger, although I might not express it that way. However, I knew that behind closed doors with my family members, I was more apt to exhibit this kind of behavior. I recognized that scenes such as those occur every day in peoples' private and business lives, as well as in physically violent ways throughout the world. Many of us have learned to handle our emotions in this manner, not realizing that there might be a better way.

Attack, blame, defend; we have held the belief that these give us power, that this is the way to get what we want. If someone isn't listening, just raise our voice, point our finger, get mad! If someone is yelling at us, just yell louder. Maybe then we will finally get our point across, or be able to defend ourselves when attacked. Of course, we all know that this doesn't get us anywhere. It may motivate others to do what we want, out of fear, but in the end, it fails to create peace or harmony between us—only intimidation, anger, withdrawal, guilt, defense, and so forth. At times, we strike out anyway, or, at least, think about it. Although it may feel good at first, the feeling is temporary, and then we ache inside because nothing has been resolved and we're upset that we lack control over our emotions.

Attacking, blaming, and defending are learned behaviors, learned attitudes. These are the ways in which many people have learned to handle their feelings. At their source is the conviction that people are flawed, that *we* are flawed. Yes, our personality (lower self) has some learning to do, but our core is untouched, perfect love and goodness. When we are seeing through the eyes of attack, blame, and defend, we are seeing only the lower self, which is merely struggling to evolve. We see wrongful behavior and, through our judgments, we promote guilt, both in the other person and then in us.

The real truth is that people are doing the best they can with what they know. If they knew better, they'd do better. People are not flawed. They are already whole and beautiful at their core, by virtue of their Divine nature, but they can't yet see it. People attack others because they are feeling fearful, hurt, guilty, threatened, or wounded. We become defensive and angry when we have been chided, criticized, condemned, or attacked. Once we have become defensive, we lash back at the other person or at ourselves. And so the cycle of attack and defend persists. It's as though fuel has been poured on an already blazing fire.

Attack, blame, and defend produce separation and conflict. Connectedness and peace can be found only through the practice of forgiveness, acceptance, and love, which can be developed with the use of all of our tools. We may be resistant to changing our ways, because we haven't yet proven to ourselves that another way works. But, only by making a new choice and experimenting with it, can we find the proof for which we're searching. I am reminded of a wise statement by Paramahansa Yogananda: "When there is a fight, at least two parties are involved. So there can be no fight with you if you refuse to participate."

When we become angry, we might begin by asking ourselves what might happen if we:

Breathe deeply several times and remind ourselves that only understanding and compassion will bring us inner peace.

Find a quiet space, put our arms around ourselves, and say, "I love you, (your name), exactly the way you are. I know you're hurting, and I understand how you feel. I want you to know that I'm here for you no matter what. You are perfect the way you are."

Call a loving friend, express our feelings, and then make the choice to see differently, through the eyes of tenderness and understanding. What might our adversary be afraid of? What woundedness do we see?

Choose to listen empathetically to the other person and really *hear* what they are feeling and saying. Sometimes others can't hear us until we have really heard them. Can we be the bigger person for the sake of inner and outer peace?

Pray for the other person or mentally send them light or loving thoughts.

Pray to God for clear vision.

Review chapters 8 and 9 and then choose a tool with which to work for a while until we calm down. Harmonious communication cannot occur until one or both parties have settled down.

Choose to talk about a disagreement with a soft, calm voice and with honor and respect for the other person's point of view.

Learning new responses to argumentative and even violent situations may take time. Even after we think we have learned our lessons, we can be taken by surprise and revert back to old behavior. We will, most certainly, from time to time, find ourselves in ugly reaction to those kinds of circumstances. The question is not *whether* we lose control, but how quickly we can refocus on love, regain our composure, and quiet our emotions.

Please note that in very violent situations, we need to set firm boundaries if we are in a position to do so. Whenever possible, we must remove ourselves from harm's way as quickly as we can. Under such circumstances our fear of injury or destruction may arise, causing us to be angry, and it is of paramount importance that we do not add fuel to the fire. If there is no target for the perpetrator of violence, then the aggression will subside more rapidly. Once we are free, we can still use our tools to calm ourselves and to pray for ourselves and our antagonist.

In situations in which we cannot flee violent behavior, it is true that we may be harmed physically. However, if we can keep our minds in steady prayer for ourselves, and for our adversary, we may be able to limit the damage and emerge from the situation with fewer scars than what might have been. Remember that prayer is a powerful tool for creating light where there is darkness. Never underestimate its mighty ability!

In summary, attack, blame and defend are behaviors that are learned responses to problematic situations and can be set aside in favor of calmer, more peaceful behavioral responses. This takes time and practice to develop but is well worth the effort. We can learn to perceive ourselves and others as innocent of wrongdoing by understanding that we are each acting from our conditioning and from our present knowledge. We can learn to see ourselves and others as reacting from fear and therefore, choose to hold compassion instead of anger. We can remind ourselves often that what we hold dear is peace, not conflict, and we can choose to act from a higher, wiser place. Inner transformation is our hope for a better world.

MIRRORING AND PROJECTION

On a spiritual level, we are all connected by an invisible, Divine force, which is at the core of our being. We feel separated from each other because, to the physical eyes, we each act and look different. Yet, since we are all part of the same Divine energy pool, we are bonded in an eternal, unified oneness. Therefore, if we look at another person, we are really seeing a reflection of ourselves. Others are simply our mirrors, and they reflect back some piece of information about us. We use the mirroring principle to gain self-awareness. Emotionally charged experiences with others can show us how we treat ourselves, how we feel about some aspect of ourselves, behaviors we have hidden from view, or our deep-seated fears. By becoming more aware of our emotional reactions to others and what they mean, we can zero in on what changes we need to make within ourselves to create greater happiness and mastery over life circumstances.

Projection occurs when we decide that others are at fault, and we judge them as wrong. The source of all projection is our own self-judgment, self-unforgiveness, woundedness, or fear. We blame others for their faults because it is more comfortable to point a finger outward, than to look at the parts of ourselves we find unacceptable. Therefore, we project our anger and self-hatred onto the world. We condemn others because we believe that if they would change, we would feel better. That is giving our power to an outside source, over which we have no control, instead of being the director of our power and using it for inner transformation. We project when we are unable to see that the Universe is supplying us with the perfect relationship in which to heal and evolve.

All humans have what we might call a dark side and a light side. This is merely the lower self and the higher, wiser self. The lower self is learning to see more clearly, to come into alignment with higher self-vision. Our dark side can be referred to as our shadow side, and it is composed of all the aspects of ourselves that we keep hidden from view because of embarrassment or shame. To move into a more peaceful state is to explore and observe our shadow side. To confront our vulnerabilities is an act of courage, and is of benefit not only to us, but to the world. The object here is to accept of all parts of us, to embrace the totality of who we are.

Thus, whenever we have a negative emotional reaction to another person, we can examine what this tells us about ourselves. Where do we need healing? What inner part haven't we accepted? There are no accidents in life. Everything that happens, happens for our highest good, and occurs in order to heal us. If anything has an emotional impact on us, its purpose is to show us something about ourselves that needs forgiveness, acceptance or love. Therefore, when we are emotionally triggered in a relationship, we can choose to look inside instead of fighting, arguing, or bickering. That way, we can learn to view ourselves and others differently, and ultimately alter our reactions, producing greater harmony within the relationship.

Let's look at some examples to understand this concept better. In our first example, you find yourself irritated because your boss is constantly hounding you to clean up your desk. You may find a need to complain to your fellow co-workers, or you may suppress your angry feelings and then become ill, as the anger eats away at you. In either case, seeing your boss as your mirror may tell you something profound about yourself, and therefore offer valuable information about what you can do to change things.

First, you examine how you feel about yourself. Is it true that you have a difficult time keeping your workspace neat and organized? If so, do you judge yourself harshly for having a messy desk? Your boss is merely mirroring the feelings you already have about yourself. The answer to greater happiness lies not in becoming angry with your boss, but rather in learning to accept yourself no matter how unorganized you may be at times. Remember, you're doing the best you can, and that's good enough. If you would like to become more organized, that's fine. With a decision to do so, you can find helpful instruction or information, if needed. But more importantly, you can stop judging yourself and develop compassion for yourself, messy or neat. When this is accomplished, you may find that your boss stops hounding you, or if he continues, your reaction to him may be less emotional and more balanced.

Another example of mirroring might be found in a friend whom you find to be nontrustworthy. This friend may keep making commitments to you and breaking them, or saying one thing, but doing another. Again, you may find yourself exasperated or frustrated with this person, yet your friend may be mirroring to you something about yourself that needs uncovering.

With closer scrutiny, you may discover that you don't trust yourself. You keep making commitments to yourself, but fail to follow through. Perhaps you try to fool yourself by acting one way, but feeling very differently inside. Lashing out at your friend (projection) really doesn't resolve the situation since you do not have control over her behavior. The problem and solution always lie within you. You can then practice accepting yourself the way you are right now. Explore your fears and possible reasons that you might be this way. Hold compassion for yourself. You're functioning the best you know how. Next, you can work toward trusting yourself to a greater degree by listening to your inner guidance and respecting yourself enough to follow it. When you make decisions, you can practice acting on them and finishing what you start. You can also learn to tune in to your true feelings and express them authentically, instead of denying that they exist. With guidance, patience, and practice, self-trust will become easier for you, and you may find your outer world changing to reflect the alterations you've made inside yourself.

One last example can serve to further clarify this principle of mirroring. Perhaps you are a parent who is having difficulty getting your child to finish his basic chores around the house. It seems that your instructions are met with disregard, as if you hadn't said them at all. Once again, you become quite upset, but you decide to examine what's already inside of you that your son is reflecting.

With closer observation, you realize that the feelings that your son evokes inside of you are that you don't count, that what you have to say isn't important. When you mull this over, you can see that you feel this way about yourself. You're the one who refuses to value yourself. You're the one who cannot see your own worth. When you come to this awareness, you can then take specific steps to build your own self-esteem. Seeing a therapist, going to a support group, using positive affirmations, etc., can help you to raise your level of self-worth. When you begin to feel better about yourself, you may pleasantly find that your son begins to behave differently, or his behavior fails to arouse your anger anymore.

The mirroring principle instructs us to go beyond the attack- blame-defend mode of behavior, which seems to be prevalent in our society. Ultimately, we are each responsible for our own well-being and happiness. No one else can do it for us. Viewing relationship difficulties from the standpoint of inner transformation can give us greater mastery over our emotions and our lives in general. If we look for our reflection in others, and explore what we see, we are truly on the path to authentic power.

In conclusion, it might be helpful to look at the following chart, which clearly delineates behaviors and language that create harmony versus conflict in relationships. Perhaps, as you think about your relationships, these will resonate with you and give you some new ideas with which to experiment.

Behaviors That Cause Joining (Creating Peace and Harmony)	Behaviors That Cause Separation (Creating Conflict and Misery)
• Listening empathically • Taking responsibility for our own feelings • Acknowledging our vulnerabilities • Admitting to our shortcomings • Letting go of all expectations • Working on healing ourselves • Refraining from telling the other person what we think they are doing, thinking, or feeling • Stepping into the other person's shoes • Taking care of our own needs • Laughing together or alone • Loving and nurturing each other • Accepting any and all situations and emotions • Praying together or alone • Understanding what we can learn from each other • Focusing on the good in ourselves and each other • Expressing empathy for the other person's position • Initiating love or nurturing • Keeping our voice soft	• Refusing to listen to the other person • Blaming the other person • Numbing ourselves or striving to be "tough" • Refusing to look at our own weaknesses • Having expectations • Looking outside of us for the cause of our discomfort • Telling the other person what we think they are doing, thinking, or feeling • Refusing to see and validate the other person's point of view • Expecting the other person to fulfill all of our needs and desires • Seeing the cup a gloomy half empty • "Beating up" on ourselves • "Beating up" on each other • Resisting our emotions and our life circumstances • Denying our spiritual nature • Disregarding the meaning and purpose behind what's happening in our relationship • Focusing on what's "wrong" or "bad" • Expressing judgment about the other person's perceptions and opinions • Waiting with resentment for the other person to apologize or offer love or nurturing • Raising our voice or yelling

Phrases That Promote Peace	Words That Produce Conflict
• In my experience … • Now I understand that … • Now I see that … • What I feel is … • My perception is … • I'm sorry that … • Have I heard you correctly? • Is there anything you'd like to add?	• Should • Ought • Never • Always • Can't

LEARNING THROUGH EXPERIENCE

A. *Explore the following questions:*

1. *Who is a person with whom you have great difficulty? After reading this chapter, what might you do differently in that relationship? What do you think you can learn by having that person in your life?*
2. *Who in your life are you most judgmental toward? What are three steps you could take toward relinquishing your judgment?*
3. *Think of a time when you felt really angry. What fear, guilt, or hurt was underlying the anger?*
4. *Think of a time when some significant other person in your life was angry with you. What fear, guilt, or hurt might have been underlying his/her anger? Put yourself in his/her shoes. What might you have been feeling if you were that person?*

B. *Exercise in practicing Mirroring and Projection:*

Mirroring

Think of a person who rubs you the wrong way or pushes your emotional buttons. What specifically upsets you about the other person's behavior?

Ask yourself the following questions:

- *Is that a way that I treat or have treated any other person at any time in my life?*
- *Is that a way that I treat or have treated myself at any time in my life?*
- *Is that a way I would never act toward another for fear of*

embarrassment, shame, or anger at myself? Under different circumstances, would it be possible for me to act that way?

- *What fears does that behavior trigger in me?*
- *If I recognize that behavior to exist somewhere inside of me, what steps could I take to forgive that part of me?*
- *What does that part of me need? How could its needs be filled?*

PROJECTION

Think of a time you felt very angry toward someone. If you were really angry with yourself, what might you have been angry about?

(Clues)

- *What was happening at that time for you? What were your own circumstances, aside from what was going on with that person?*
- *If you know what you were angry about within yourself, what is one step you could take toward forgiving yourself?*

C. *Pick one or two of the following affirmations and work with them for thirty days. Observe any changes that might occur inside or outside of you.*

1. *I see only the good in __________.*
2. *I see only the good in myself.*
3. *My relationship with __________ is easy, fulfilling, respectful, and loving.*
4. *Every day, in every way, this relationship gets better and better.*
5. *The God power within me (us) is stronger than any obstacle between us.*
6. *Today I choose peace rather than conflict.*

7. *Guilt and blame are now gone, and I see only innocence in myself and _________.*
8. *I completely forgive myself for _________. I completely forgive _________ for _________.*
9. *All is well in this relationship as we continually create win-win situations.*

D. *PRAYERS from Illuminata, by Marianne Williamson*

Dear God,

Show me the light at the center of by brothers (or a particular person).
Show me the light at the center of myself.
Show me the light at the center of the world.
Where I see guilt, show me innocence.
Where I focus on mistakes, show me how to focus on efforts at good.
Help me have faith in the goodness of others (or a particular person).
Help me have faith in Your Spirit within me.
Thus may darkness be cast out.
May I cleave to the light that is my heart.
This is my prayer.
May I see the light in everyone (or someone in particular).
AMEN

Dear God,

Please reveal our love to us, for now it is obscured.
Bring us peace and healing, for we are lost in the darkness of conflict and separation.
We surrender to You our attacks and defenses.
We relinquish all perceptions that we bring from the past.
We surrender to You our positions and agendas.
Please help us see love.
Please bring us back to the path of peace.
Cleanse our minds of all but helpful thoughts.
May our relationship be reborn through Your Spirit and grace.
We apologize for: (say your own).
We forgive the following: (say your own).
Please clear our path that we might see again, the light that is our love for each other.
Thank you very much.
AMEN

The "connective" tissue within the new form of business
is full of heart, made up of caring, concern,
and a willingness to be as helpful
to others as we would like others to be to us.
It is a consciousness focused on giving
rather than on getting and a self-realization that
comes when we do everything we can to empower
everyone to be the most she or he can be.
—Gerald Jampolsky, MD and Diane Cirincione

Chapter 16

Work and School

MY older sister, in my childhood perception, was always smarter and more talented than I was. Her grades were constantly higher than mine, and she loved to read, which I did not. That latter skill provided her with a rich and deep vocabulary, which I felt I lacked. Even small incidents reminded me of her greater success. I remember once in seventh grade taking a required home economics class and trying to make an apron, which was not my forte. When I found myself having trouble with the stitching, I asked my teacher for help, only to hear the remark, "Can't you do anything better than your sister?" Needless to say, that reinforced my notion that I was worthless and others were simply more gifted than I. Certainly, most teachers these days are not so blunt or unkind. Yet, the tendency to compare one person to another, and to judge them unfairly, persists in the educational and occupational arenas, sometimes secretly or subtly, and sometimes overtly.

In Western culture, from the time we are small, we are indoctrinated into the world of school as preparation for working as a solid and contributing citizen of our country. As youngsters, our environment consists of classrooms within our schools (unless we are home schooled) and our "work" is our studies. As we become older, we shift into the world of jobs, careers, or professions, in which we earn a living in whatever field we've chosen. Work is an integral part of each of our lives, and we spend much of our time and energy there.

If our work environment is healthy, and we are accepted and shown appreciation for what we can offer, we thrive. However, if we are criticized, judged excessively, compared to another, or presented with unrealistic expectations, we may fail to thrive, especially if we believe what we are told and take it as a sign that we are unworthy.

Regrettably, our school systems are set up to pass some, fail others, praise and reward students with high grades, overlook those with mediocre grades, and punish those with low grades. Our school curriculum is often dictated by governmental guidelines, which ignore our individuality, in favor of teaching knowledge and skills, which correlate to the talents of only "mainstream" youngsters. As students, we constantly find ourselves in competitive positions, vying to be good, better, best, or at least acceptable in the minds of our teachers, parents, and friends.

The corporate world is often an extension of this educational environment with its emphasis on financial gain, greater (bigger and better) productivity, and impersonal pink slips. Small business owners often feel the pressure to grow larger (bigger and better) and to survive in a world of competitive struggle. That pressure is passed down to employees as an attitude, an imperative of operation. In addition, since every line of work is a business of some type, needing to produce a sturdy and profitable living for its workers, such attitudes persist far and wide, in every profession, in every occupation.

As adults, the reality is that we *do* have to make a living to support ourselves and our loved ones. Yet, we often focus our energy in a nonproductive place. Centering our attention on financial gain only is treating the symptom alone, which may or may not work, but most certainly does not create long-term stability. Concentrating on prestige/status or success/failure, inflates or deflates our self-worth, and separates us from others, causing a lonely and undesirable existence. Under such conditions, our stress levels and productivity decrease, producing burnout, sickness, and higher absenteeism.

The reality is that acceptance, love, patience, generosity, and respect, etc., are elements that promote health in the workplace, producing greater contentment among workers. Increased morale, job excitement, personal power, optimism, and productivity are additional effects. When there is no expectation for any person to perform like another, and each individual is valued and honored for their particular skills, job satisfaction, efficiency, and financial gain begin to rise. When mistakes are seen as learning opportunities for everyone involved, and then forgiven, it is easier to correct course and move forward. All school systems and work systems are made up of individuals, and, when these individuals thrive, so does the system. It seems to me that our greatest strength is our ability to change the way we view ourselves and others so that we see everyone through the eyes of nonjudgment, forgiveness, connection, and consideration. Only then can our schools and places of work be safe, satisfying, and productive environments for all.

Toward that end, the following discussions are meant to evoke thoughtful deliberation.

NEW PERCEPTIONS

As we know now, the thoughts and beliefs we hold have a powerful and direct effect on our feelings and actions. Perceptions we have about ourselves, our world, and the people in it, can make us or break us. And as we've discussed, healing into peace is all about shifting perceptions of what we see. Therefore, uprooting destructive perceptions and replacing them with beneficial ones can be enormously productive and greatly therapeutic.

Some time ago I had a conversation with a businessman who was a manager at a large company. He mentioned that the company was downsizing, and that many of the people whom he supervised, and had grown to know and care for, were going to be devastated by the inevitable job losses looming in the near future. He was the one who had to make the decisions about who stayed and who left, and he felt badly about having to let go of any of his workers, even though some of them did higher quality work than others.

The encounter led me to contemplate a variety of workplace (and school life) scenarios that could be viewed in a more peaceful way. Below are listed several of these scenarios with old commonplace perceptions listed, as well as possible new ways of "seeing." I have found that in most cases these new perceptions are freeing and open us to the good intention of the Universe, bringing us comfort during difficult times.

1. **Scenario**: I get laid off from my job.

   Old Perceptions: I'm a failure and a loser.

   New Perceptions: I didn't like this job anyway. The Universe must be creating a work situation that uses my talents and gifts more effectively. A new job may be much more enjoyable. Or, I haven't really enjoyed the people I've been working with. I'm being moved into a new environment where there are people with whom I have more in common, and with whom I'm supposed to work for some reason. Or, I have always worried about having enough money. The Divine is asking me to trust and know that I will be led to prosperity because the Universe is totally abundant, and I need to learn that truth.

2. **Scenario**: My boss (teacher) criticizes me almost every day, even for seemingly insignificant reasons.

   Old Perceptions: I must be incapable and stupid.

   New Perceptions: My boss (teacher) is unhappy in his home situation, and is unable to deal directly with his feelings. Or, my boss (teacher) is very hard on himself and his inner critic sees himself in me. Or, my boss (teacher) is mirroring the way that I always talk to myself. I am super self-critical, and need to work on loving myself more.

3. **Scenario**: My co-worker (friend) is really getting on my nerves. She talks to me constantly, and I can't get my work done.

   Old Perceptions: I feel so guilty when I get irritable, but I really feel angry with her, and angry at myself for feeling that way.

   New Perceptions: My mother has been sick, and I've been taking care of her every evening and on the weekends. I'm really tired, and I need to forgive myself for my moodiness and get some sleep. Or, I have never been able to set boundaries for myself and be assertive. I need to learn to let go of my fear of speaking up to other people when I need to, and learn healthy ways of communicating my needs. That's why this is happening in my life.

4. **Scenario**: One of the workers I manage continually comes in late to work and slacks off during the day. I don't want to fire him because I know he needs the money.

Old Perceptions: I always seem to find myself in a place where I feel like the bad guy. Something must be wrong with me.

New Perceptions: The Universe wants to teach me healthy and appropriate ways to deliver negative feedback. There are loving and unloving ways to confront others about their behavior, and I can investigate and choose to do this kindly. Or, I want everyone to like me, and I fear that any criticism, no matter how constructive, will turn my employees against me. I am being taught that my worth is not based upon others' opinions of me. Or, this worker may not be suited for this job. He may function better in a different department, or a different job.

5. **Scenario**: I can't seem to concentrate on my work lately.

   Old Perceptions: What's wrong with me? I'm not performing my responsibilities. I don't deserve this job (I shouldn't even stay in school). I'm not good enough!

   New Perceptions: My life has been chaotic lately. My daughter has needed me to help her move and baby-sit for her kids, my husband has just retired and seems to want my company all the time, and my father's health has been failing. I need to forgive myself and be loving to myself during this stressful time. Or, I've had a lot on my mind lately, especially since my boyfriend dumped me. Maybe I need to see a counselor to sort out all of this. Maybe I just need to give myself time to grieve and ease up on myself. Or, I've been working on this project for a long time now. It's okay to rest a bit before going on. Or, I've been at this job for twenty-five years. Maybe the Universe is trying to tell me it's time to retire.

Looking at our lives differently requires that we let go of old habitual ways of thinking, and honor ourselves enough to consider new ideas. Because our thoughts are powerful creators of feeling, what's in our minds is of the utmost importance in altering our moods. Therefore, allowing new beliefs and perceptions to enter our consciousness is a gift we give to ourselves and then to everyone we encounter. As we gain greater peace of mind, our schoolmates or co-workers are our beneficiaries, for our own peace of mind is contagious, and a blessing to all.

COMPETITION

Competition, comparison, evaluation, etc., have been part of human existence since ancient times. As we have discussed, we are always rating ourselves and others, devising systems that will serve to judge our worth, as well as the worth of friends, other students, and other workers. We can't seem to help ourselves, and yet the anxiety, which we create through this process, is certainly painful and unwanted. Sometimes it's a giant headache!

I remember when my son hit a home run in high school baseball. When he brought in three runs, we were all ecstatic, but when he was injured or in a batting slump, I worried about how he would react and how the other players would treat him. I also wondered whether I was in favor of school athletics as we know them, with such pressure to win. Do we hang onto our competitiveness for the high that comes with beating our opponent? Do we keep comparing ourselves with others because of the sudden worth we feel when all goes well and we do better than the next guy? Are we afraid that we will lose all our motivation if we give up our competitiveness?

Somehow, we find ourselves believing that our self-worth is based upon what we do in life, rather than on who we are, children of Divinity, love, and goodness. We forget that we are naturally creative beings and that our creative urges exist innately, without a competitive push. To become conscious of these truths is to feel the harmony and peace of joining with our fellow man instead of feeling the anxiety and fear of separateness.

I believe we live in a world of competition in order to experience the feeling of separateness. All experiences in this world are instructive to us and teach us how to obtain the peacefulness and connection that we've forgotten. Sometimes we can't know what we are looking for unless we meet with its opposite. For example, the murderer cannot know fully that she wishes not to kill until she experiences how she feels when she acts in such a way. A student (or worker) who constantly complains will not learn to see the good in things until he eventually sees the painful futility of looking only at the negative. He must suffer to change his ways, it seems. And those who hold a grudge against the world or against another person cannot know peace until they become fed up with the repeated feelings of being resentful.

Thus it is with competition. Undergoing opposition and rivalry is a necessary part of the cleansing or purification process leading to a clear knowingness that this kind of living leads not to feelings of wellness, but to feelings of anxiety and discomfort. It seems we must live this repeatedly to master the lesson. We either condemn the competitive bent of our world or we praise its efficacy in keeping us on track. But no matter what we think of competition, we often find ourselves embroiled in it, without consciously scrutinizing its effects upon us. If we can become aware of the separating and oppositional qualities of competition, and how that feels inside of us, we will ultimately work together to create win-win situations and cooperative work communities.

MOVING INTO THE FUTURE

The problems and challenges that face us in schools, corporations, industrial work, small businesses, and institutions are multifaceted and certainly cannot be discussed within the parameters of this book. However, human beings are writing the template. The higher our consciousness and the more we are able to think and act from a place of caring, respect, and knowledge of Universal law, the more effective we will be.

Already, some educational programs are transforming to include cooperative learning, hands-on experiences and less focus on grades with more on learning motivation, learning satisfaction, and learning quality. Programs have arisen that look at individual learning styles and capacities while examining the cultural effects of absorbing and understanding educational material. In some places the arts are being given the attention and esteem that they deserve, and wellness programs are beginning to gain popularity, with youngsters, parents, and teachers. Conflict resolution has become a part of high school extra curriculum with peer mediators functioning to help fellow students with disputes.

Some corporations and institutions have begun to offer their employees a wider array of resources, including mental health–related seminars, workout gyms, psychologists on-site, bonding activities, and the like. Some of the most successful businesses are headed by employers who are in touch with the needs of their employees and aim to make certain that the office environment is a desirable and friendly place to be.

I believe that as we move forward into the future, we must work to create learning and work atmospheres that most fully operate to unlock the Divine creativity of our parents, teachers, students, bosses, and employees. In that vein, the following prayers are offered in the hope that we can build more successful, harmonic, and prosperous environments for all.

1. In any interaction, may we think of two or more people, not just ourselves.
2. May we practice listening to others.
3. May we practice listening to and speaking from our hearts.

4. When we are upset, may we be brave enough to take responsibility for our feelings, instead of attacking another.
5. May we work to find win-win solutions to problems that arise.
6. When we disagree with another, if no solution is found, may we agree to disagree, honoring another's perception.
7. May we remember that all troubling experiences are the perfect ones for our soul growth.
8. May we always look to understand the lessons in our difficulties.
9. May we realize that we are in this together and work to see the commonalities between us rather than the differences.

LEARNING THROUGH EXPERIENCE

A. *As always, explore these questions and see if you can learn anything new about yourself at work or in school.*

1. *How accepting are you of others' "mistakes"? How accepting are you of yours?*
2. *How is your patience with others at school (or work)? How is your patience with yourself?*
3. *How might you increase your respect for others and for yourself? What key words or thoughts can remind you to honor another? To honor yourself?*
4. *What do you need in order to let your creativity soar?*
5. *Choose a situation at school or work that bothers you. How might you perceive this differently? That is, in a positive, meaningful way?*
6. *How do you deal with competition? What can it teach you?*

B. *What is your vision for your present school or work environment? Make a list of what you perceive to be needed improvements? How would they be implemented? Be as detailed as you possibly can. What do you like about your school or work environment?*

C. *What is your ideal job? Visualize yourself happy and fulfilled in your perfect work situation?*

1. *What would you like to be doing?*
2. *Who would you want to be near you?*
3. *Who would you want to work with?*
4. *What does your work environment look like?*

5. *How would you like to respond to someone who's irritable or critical? What can you learn from that person? See yourself in such a situation acting calm, capable and skilled. Practice, practice, practice.*

D. *When you are angry at someone in school or work:*

1. *Pause and take time to consider all possible responses before acting poorly. Ask a trusted friend or advisor for options or make a list of options beforehand and keep the list in your desk and close at hand.*
2. *Ask yourself if you are angry at yourself for something. If so tell yourself that you're doing the best you can.*
3. *Remind yourself that this person is doing the best he/she can too.*

E. *Choose to examine or observe the person you most dislike at school or work.*

1. *What might that person be afraid of?*
2. *What woundedness might motivate that person to act poorly? What do you know about him or her?*
3. *What might that person need?*

F. *Pick one or two of the following affirmations and practice each 20 times/day for a month. See if it makes a difference for you.*

1. *I am secure, safe, and abundant every day of my life, and I work at a job that I enjoy.*
2. *I can handle any challenge that arises at work (school).*
3. *I choose compassion and respect for my fellow co-workers (students).*

4. *I work in a harmonious, friendly environment in which everyone gets along with each other.*
5. *I am my most creative self at work (school).*

Forgiveness is the fragrance
that the violet sheds on
the heel that has crushed it.
—Mark Twain

CHAPTER 17

Forgiveness

IN April of 2005, I had just finished my work as program chairperson at a nonviolence conference in Detroit where I live. For a year and a half, I had lived, breathed, and dreamed about nonviolence philosophy, wanting to understand it in depth and attempting to pull together an enlightened and inspiring group of presenters. One of those presenters turned out to be a close and dear friend of mine with whom I'd had years of collaborative teaching and working. Diane taught a workshop on Thursday morning, and I hugged her when she came in, only to say that I'd hook up with her at the end of the morning when I wasn't so busy. But by morning's end I'd missed her, as she had other commitments that afternoon.

I was exhausted by the end of the conference on Friday and had a hectic weekend coming up. I swore I would call her on Monday morning to thank her for presenting and to touch base. Early Monday morning, however, I received a phone call from her alarm company (I was on her list to call in case of emergency), saying there was alleged trouble at Diane's house. Unfortunately, she lived quite a distance from me, so I was of no help. A short time later I received a phone call from another good friend who informed me that Diane had been murdered, and it was all over the news. Her mother had found her body wedged against the front door. Shocking as this was, the greatest jolt came later, as we found out that Diane's son, age fifteen, had committed this horrific crime by stabbing his mother repeatedly.

I had known her son, Christopher, since he was a toddler—a slightly built, sweet child who loved to play computer games and read books. As he grew into his teen years, Chris would often be found on his computer, and unbeknownst to his parents, apparently in response to inner conflict, he had discovered some frightening, cultish websites, which portrayed "new age practitioners" as the enemy. Diane was anything but conservative and her more liberal mind-set may have triggered condemnation in the eyes of a very confused fifteen-year-old. To this day, we'll never know exactly what set him off, but Chris lost control and killed his beloved mom. Some think he lost touch with reality, some believe he knew exactly what he was doing, but after his initial stay in prison, Christopher came to the conclusion that he had committed a terrible wrong and that he needed to be punished for what he did. He gave up the choice to plead insanity and instead pleaded guilty as charged. He now faces twenty-five to thirty years in prison.

Diane had taught forgiveness classes and workshops for years and had raised her son as a single parent, while working to make a living for them both. Unfortunately, she didn't see this coming until it was too late. Those who knew her remarked that this was probably the greatest test of forgiveness her soul had ever known. And yet, we all agreed that, had Diane lived, she would have most definitely pleaded with everyone to forgive her son. I'm certain that she firmly believed Christopher had momentarily lost all rational thought, had been led astray, and was doing the best he could do with his raw, adolescent, troubled state of mind. Those of us who knew Diane were deeply affected by her murder and equally bewildered by the circumstances. Yet, each of us too, had been given the challenge of forgiving Chris by perceiving his youthful ignorance and inner turmoil.

Because much of our world still lives in fear-based consciousness, forgiveness is not always endorsed as a positive or useful practice. As a species, we still struggle with an enormous amount of anger, which is an outgrowth of our fear and pain. This is only because we haven't yet realized the truth of our connectedness.

As a consequence, the custom of forgiveness is not always popular, and even with good intention, we are often drawn back into the unforgiving mode of thought. Forgiveness is frequently a long and arduous task, but it is our salvation as a world. Not only is it possible within each of us, but it is essential to a global community that faces conflict on a daily basis.

Author and physician, Gerald Jampolsky, remarks,

> *From the perspective of love and Spirit, forgiveness is the willingness to let go of the hurtful past. It is the decision to no longer suffer, to heal your heart and soul. It is the choice to no longer find value in hatred or anger. And it is letting go of the desire to hurt others or ourselves because of something that is already in the past. It is the willingness to open our eyes to the light in other people rather than to judge or condemn them.*

In this view of forgiveness, we can see its utmost importance to the healing of our planet. It can begin right here with us, and work its way into the fabric of societal norms, if enough of us are committed to its promise. It is my hope that the following discussions will ignite the flame of intention within each of us so that we can more easily steer our way through the particulars of such a difficult but rewarding practice.

FORGIVENESS AS A BOOMERANG

When we're angry and wounded, forgiveness may be the last thing on our mind. We may ask ourselves why we should pardon such a terrible person or cruel act. Forgiveness may seem to be most irrational and unfair in that moment. However, if we realize that the practice of forgiveness is a boomerang, we motivate ourselves to think differently. By this I mean that what we put out into the Universe comes back to us. This, as you may recall, is a law of the cosmos. When we truly forgive from our hearts, the goodness and compassion we emit, returns to us in a multitude of ways. First, and foremost, we feel peaceful on the inside. We feel whole and full and contented. In addition, the Universe mirrors our lovingness by causing our lives to flow smoothly and easily. This happens because the practice of forgiveness is in alignment with Universal purpose. Thus, we forgive for ourselves first, but we most certainly benefit others in the process.

The following e-mail, which depicts this idea, was sent to me anonymously, a few years ago. It was titled, *A Heavy Load.*

> *One of my teachers had each one of us bring a clear bag and a sack of potatoes to school. For every person we'd refuse to forgive in our life experience, we were told to choose a potato, write on it the name and date, and put it in the plastic bag. Some of our bags, as you can imagine, were quite heavy.*
>
> *We were then told to carry this bag with us everywhere for one week, putting it beside our bed at night, on the car seat when driving, next to our desk at work. The hassle of lugging this around with us made it clear what a weight we were carrying spiritually, and how we had to pay attention to it all the time to not forget, and keep leaving it in embarrassing places.*
>
> *Naturally, the condition of the potatoes deteriorated to nasty slime. This*

was a great metaphor for the price we pay for keeping our pain and heavy negativity!

Too often we think of forgiveness as a gift to the other person, and it clearly is for ourselves! So the next time you decide you can't forgive someone, ask yourself, isn't your bag heavy enough?

FUNDAMENTALS OF FORGIVENESS

At times there is great confusion over what it means to forgive. Some think they are forgiving when they are really holding onto anger. Others avoid forgiveness for fear they will have to then be in close contact with the recipient of their forgiveness. I've known those who forgive conditionally with the expectation that the other person do what they want and others who believe that forgiveness means they must take some further action, and so on. The following fundamentals of forgiveness may help us to understand better the particulars of this courageous practice. Ironically, Diane and I created this list together before she died.

1. **Forgiveness is the ability to see with the eyes of the heart, not the physical eyes.** It is not an intellectual task, but rather, an internal feeling and perception that exudes compassion and understanding.

2. **Forgiveness is a process and can have many layers or degrees.** Forgiveness unfolds for us as we become willing to see ourselves and others differently. We may feel at one point that we have forgiven a particular person and at a later date, feel anger toward them again. This merely means that there is another layer of anger (and fear) to release.

3. **When an immediate situation seems impossible to forgive, it points to a root cause in the soul's past experience.** We must express and release feelings associated with these experiences before we can forgive completely. We must choose safe places to do this work in order to reap the benefits.

4. **Through the continuous act of surrender, we allow the God-Force to work with our minds and our hearts to change our misperceptions.** Forgiveness is grace. It is given to us by Spirit, as we connect with Infinite Intelligence and allow ourselves to follow our Divine guidance.

5. **Forgiveness does not require us to take any outward action unless we are inwardly guided to do so.** Forgiveness is an attitude—an energy output that is not visually seen but rather felt. There are no requirements to befriend, support, or speak frequently to this person. If action of some sort is to ..be taken, it is felt on the inside as a knowingness, not a "should."

6. **Forgiveness does not mean condoning or approving of someone's poor behavior.** We do not need to agree with what this person has done. We must only understand and hold compassion for their actions. For example, we can help to send a criminal to prison but still have empathy for him.

7. **Forgiveness does not rule out setting boundaries and protecting ourselves if need be.** When we find ourselves in harm's way, we must be cognizant of our own well-being. Setting physical or verbal boundaries, removing ourselves from the situation, or using force when absolutely necessary are not indications of an inability to forgive. True forgiveness may or may not be possible in a moment

of crisis, but again, forgiveness is only a feeling of empathy deep within, not an action.

8. **Forgiveness has no expectations as to the behavior of the other person.** We do not forgive to elicit a certain behavior from the other party. We forgive to feel happier, lighter, and more connected. When we expect something in return, we block these inner sensations.

9. **Forgiveness can be done in silence, having no requirement for announcement.** Sometimes we feel we have to "speak our truth," or it doesn't count. There are occasions when this is helpful, and others when it is not. We must discern whether our audience is open to this kind of thinking. If they are not, we may cause ourselves more harm and create deeper chasms between us. If they are, talk of forgiveness may help to alleviate their pain or teach a beautiful truth.

10. **When we are not feeling forgiving, we are in a state of fear and needing help from God, others whom we trust, or ourselves.** Remember that fear underlies anger. If we are feeling betrayed, intimidated, criticized, or the like, what real fears live inside of us? Are we afraid that we're not good enough, that we will be physically or emotionally harmed, that we won't be able to handle our emotions, that we will die, or that we will be alone? We must examine our fears and ask for the help that we need from the appropriate sources.

11. **The act of forgiveness can plant seeds in the consciousness of others even though they may not be able to follow suit at this time.** To forgive is to model behavior for another. On some energetic level, the person who is the object of forgiveness absorbs the

pardon and learns from it. It may not be apparent to us, but it has made a difference.

12. **The process of forgiveness requires support from like minds.** Because forgiveness is not always recognized as a "correct" or "positive" practice, it helps to have similarly minded people in our corner. Through friendly support, we can more easily shift our perceptions.

13. **Forgiveness has a balancing effect on our physical bodies.** Our "sack of rotten potatoes" can wreak havoc with our physical bodies, sending us to doctors, hospitals, and more. For example, many cancer patients have discovered hidden, internal reservoirs of anger, and persons with auto-immune diseases are often full of self-unforgiveness.

14. **Forgiveness does not mean pretending that the situation didn't happen. That is denial.** Often, we're so uncomfortable with another's unkind act, that we choose to stop thinking about and dealing with our feelings. We go about our lives as though nothing hurtful happened, and yet we feel anxious, uneasy or apprehensive. We may become addicted to any number of outside influences in order to cope.

15. **Forgiveness is letting go of past judgmental perceptions, and is, therefore, a present moment choice to see innocence and to experience peace of mind.** We always have a choice of how to handle troublesome situations. Sometimes, it is just to pause and remind ourselves of the other person's, or our own, woundedness. If further action is needed, we can choose to follow our guidance until we are able to forgive.

16. **The mirroring principle says that whatever behavior we have not forgiven within ourselves, will ultimately be perpetrated upon another, if not overtly, silently.** This is why it is so important to work on self-forgiveness. The more we see ourselves through the eyes of compassion, the more we will be able to view another in the same way. If we feel unforgiving toward another, it is a sure bet that we are feeling unforgiving toward ourselves.

17. **Forgiveness permits us to let go of all thoughts that tend to separate us from each other.** Separation causes fear, isolation, and loneliness. Forgiveness generates a peaceful connectedness.

18. **Forgiveness ends the illusion of separation, and its power can change misery into happiness in one second.** The act of forgiveness is so powerful and in such great alignment with Universal intention that its rewards are swift and grand.

FORGIVENESS AS A PROCESS

As mentioned in the previous section, forgiveness can be seen as a process, one in which we release layers of hurt, anger, and fear over a period of time. Sometimes present-moment happenings trigger old soul memories, which are already emotion-laden. When this happens, our response to a negative situation—a comment, a betrayal, a rejection—can feel quite powerful and even threaten to overwhelm us. Most likely, in such a case, we have built up multiple layers of emotion and, because we have not known how to handle these feelings in a healthy manner, the energy around such encounters has intensified. It often takes repetition of a hurtful circumstance to remove all the layers of negativity and to see clearly.

Over the years, I worked on forgiving my father for his severe judgment of me, and often I came to a place of peace for a while. Then, when I least expected it, something again would trigger my father's voice inside of me, and I'd be right back in my fear and anger. When I was younger, I would become frustrated and think to myself that I would never feel forgiveness for him. However, I've come to understand that I was just stripping away layers of built-up emotion from childhood and probably from earlier soul experiences as well. As I've been persistent in my personal growth efforts, heavy emotion, sparked by "fatherlike" situations, has greatly diminished. Forgiveness for Dad comes much easier to me than in the past.

Likewise, self-forgiveness, which has been difficult for me, has increased over time. For example, forgiving myself for my earlier addictions to alcohol, tranquilizers, and food, took many years. I was so full of shame over my lack of control and self-centeredness, that it took much emotional release work to free me of my own inner critic. But, with time, I've eased up on myself and come to the realization that I did as best I could with what I knew back then.

I find that the more horrific the act of perpetration, the longer it can take to forgive. For some, Christopher's criminal act produced an outrage so great that the pardoning process may be long and arduous, and forgiveness may or may not occur in this lifetime. I was spared this, because I had known Chris ever since he was a sweet little boy. I knew his essence, and I saw only a confused, frightened adolescent. But for others I know, this act seemed reprehensible, unforgivable, and beyond repair. Only with much expression of feeling and inner shifting of perception, will they be able to forgive.

When we have been highly abused, neglected, or treated unjustly, forgiveness takes a longer time. This can happen individually or collectively, such as in the case of 9/11. The crimes committed by Osama Bin Laden, Saddam Hussein, and Hitler are hard to forgive. Those misdeeds were so entirely antithetical to Universal purpose, and they affected so many people, that their power to harm dug deeply into the psyche of the world. Only on an individual basis can each of us work to reclaim an accurate vision of the humanity of these men and their armies. This process may seem impossible, and yet, as members of the human race and God's living kingdom, these men are part of us, and their actions an outgrowth of the collective consciousness of our planet. Given time, perseverance, and enough effort, hopefully we will be able to see their essence and realize that their acts presented lessons for us. Such deeds can demonstrate to us the judgments and prejudices of our joint and personal consciousness, which must be rectified.

Mahatma Ghandi said, "If we practice an eye for an eye and a tooth for a tooth, soon the whole world will be blind and toothless." We must ask ourselves, sometimes over and over again, if this is the direction we want to take. Peace can be found only through the practice of forgiveness and seeing clearly the goodness and the vulnerability in our fellow man. We must be patient with ourselves. Forgiveness develops over time with support, appropriate expression of feeling, and firm resolve. We can move forward, as we embrace the forgiveness process, by continuing to remind ourselves of the deep and satisfying peace to be found there, and of the enormous influence that our forgiving mind can wield in a world that is burdened by conflict. As author and theologian, Lewis B. Smedes, has stated:

> *With a little more time and a little more insight, we begin to see both ourselves and our enemies in humbler profiles.... We do not usually have a gigantic monster to forgive; we have a weak, needy, and somewhat stupid human being. When you see your enemy and yourself in the weakness and silliness of the humanity you share, it will make the miracle of forgiving a little easier.*

Forgiveness can spawn forgiveness. When we touch someone with a forgiving heart, they feel accepted and innocent. When this occurs, they are freed from the burden of shame and guilt. They can open, then, to extend themselves to others in the same way, and those they affect will touch new people, and so forth. That is why the act of forgiveness is so powerful. It holds the seed for the healing of the world. So we must understand that our one small act of pardon is not so small. It has the potential to influence thousands of people . For others and ourselves, it is worth our time and effort to remember this great truth and to learn this miraculous practice.

LEARNING THROUGH EXPERIENCE

A. *Explore these questions:*

1. *Who is one person (group of people) that you need to forgive and why?*
2. *What gift has this person (group of people) given you by being in your life?*
3. *What would motivate you to give up your anger and look upon that person with compassion?*
4. *What do you need to forgive yourself for?*
5. *What do you need in order to forgive yourself?*
6. *What is your next step in your forgiveness process?*

B. *Guided meditation on Forgiveness:*

Read this in small increments, feeding yourself the words, and then closing your eyes and visualizing whatever comes to mind: (The word he has been used for simplification. Feel free to change it to she. You may also use yourself as the object of your anger.)

Relax yourself in a way that works best for you. It helps to breathe deeply for a few minutes, moving your mind slowly away from the outer world. When you feel ready, begin.

Take a moment to visualize yourself in a place that feels sacred to you. It can be a beach, a wooded alcove, by a stream, a holy room, or the like. As you sit quietly in this hallowed spot, see a great white light coming toward you, and growing as it approaches you. When it comes very close, allow it to encircle you, embracing you in its warmth and glow. It is safe to be here, and you know that the God of your choice is here watching over you.

Now there appears before you a person in whose presence you feel anger. Because this is a safe and protected place, you are free to express yourself directly to this person and tell him why you are angry. Do it now. Speak from your heart and tell him what you feel and why. See this person really listening to you and hearing what you say.

When you feel that he has heard you, ask him to tell you how he feels and what has compelled him to act in such a way. At this moment he is his most genuine self and speaks to you in his most vulnerable way. Listen carefully so that you may take in the truth of his words.

Now, if you can, tell him that you forgive him and give him a big, wonderful gift. If you feel able, move close to him and give him a warm hug. If you have trouble doing this, move as close to him as you feel able. Perhaps touch hands or smile, whatever you are able to do.

Next, stand facing each other and watch as your spirits rise from your bodies and join. Move away from your bodies and watch them turn to shells. A cleansing river of water comes then and washes the shells away.

As spirits, you now feel your oneness and the tenderness and warmth that was always there, though previously hidden. Love him. Feel the love he has for you. Implant this image firmly upon your consciousness and, when you're ready, open your eyes, ready to take your new understanding with you out into the world.

The effort to link power with compassion
tends to bring concern for spiritual growth
and social action together, where they belong.
—*George Dole*

CHAPTER 18

Putting It All Together

WHEN I was a little girl, I used to say my prayers every night before I went to sleep. I would pray for my family members, my friends, and my teachers, but the more I prayed, the more I realized how many people there were who needed God's blessings and protection. I would extend my thoughts to everyone I knew and then to all those I had never met, from states and countries far away. Next came the animals, the trees, and the insects. It seemed that my list was never ending, for I would touch on one group of people or species and then think of another. Deep within, I felt the compulsion to help the earth and all of its inhabitants. I wanted to make a difference, and yet I didn't know how. The task seemed too daunting. This longing stayed with me through much of my life as I struggled to understand this inner mission that nagged at me.

As I've aged, my perspective has been enhanced by what I've learned along the way and by the realization that all I needed to do was to follow my inner guidance, which continuously led me to open my heart to love. Because love's nature is that it must be shared, I began to recognize that I was doing my part all along the way, just by revisiting empathy, kindness, honor, and appreciation, which already existed inside of me, waiting to be discovered. Anytime I was working toward that end, I was helping to heal the world and everyone in it.

Dr. David Hawkins, in his remarkable book, *Power vs. Force*, tells us:

> *The only way to enhance one's power in the world is by increasing one's integrity, understanding, and capacity for compassion. If diverse populations of mankind can be brought to this realization, the survival of human society and the happiness of its members is secure.*

I concur with Dr. Hawkins's vision and, moreover, I believe that those of us who are able must act as stewards of this world. I trust that each one of us has the amazing capacity to influence the whole of which we are a part. Whether we join other social activists in group efforts to effect change, whether we benevolently reach out to others one person at a time, or whether we work on our own healing, we can each make a difference. We cannot open our hearts to love without affecting all whom we touch. We are visible examples—models and teachers—for all beings with whom we come into contact, and on an energetic thought level, for even those with whom we may never have interaction. The consciousness of mankind rises through our individual willingness and effort to discover our center of love, for love's power is greater than any other force on this planet.

Humans are in a unique position within the animal kingdom. Only we can consciously choose our thoughts and actions. For generations and generations human beings have struggled to make sense out of their existence and have suffered in order to find happiness, purpose, meaning, and connection. Through a process of trial and error, we have found out what *doesn't* work. Warring, control, manipulation, abuse of power, argument, anger, withdrawal, fear—none of those has solved the puzzle.

But those of us who have tasted love, kindness, understanding, and compassion know its mighty capacity to heal and to bring us together in a fashion unlike any other. Using those attributes, we come to know joy, we are given purpose, and we bond with one another. everything for which mankind has searched for so long. Through love we can improve the lives of the generations that follow us, of all those who inherit the earth. We can better ensure the safety of our children and grandchildren, and although the choice for love may require us to change our ways, the answer to all of Earth's conflicts sit before us, simply, quietly waiting for us in all of its shining glory.

One of my older son's favorite quotes, plastered at the bottom of all his e-mails, catches my attention every time he sends me something. Written by Anita Roddick, it says, "If you think you're too small to make a difference, you've never been in bed with a mosquito." No, we're not mosquitoes, but if we were, and our bite oozed love, imagine what we could do.

LEARNING THROUGH EXPERIENCE

The following is based upon the Buddhist lovingkindness meditation, also known as Metta meditation. Included are a longer version and then a shorter one if time constraints are an issue. Feel free to use whatever lines speak to you, or create your own. Metta has been used as an antidote to all negative emotions and as a tool to help us realize that we are a part of the web of life and that all life is interconnected and interdependent. It is a means for joining, for unification, and for peace.

Lovingkindness Meditation

May I be filled with lovingkindness; may I be held in lovingkindness.
May I accept myself just as I am.
May I be free from danger, worry, tension, anger, and fear.
May I have courage and confidence.
May I be happy and healthy.
May I touch great and natural peace.
May I know the joy of being alive.
May my life be of benefit to all beings.
May my heart and mind awaken; may I be free.

(For the next verse, first choose someone who is easy for you to love, then someone who is more difficult.)

May you be filled with lovingkindness; may you be held in lovingkindness.
May you accept yourself just as you are.
May you be free from danger, worry, tension, anger, and fear.
May you have courage and confidence.
May you be happy and healthy.

May you touch great and natural peace.
May you know the joy of being alive.
May your life be of benefit to all beings.
May your heart and mind awaken; may you be free.

May all beings be filled with lovingkindness; may all beings be held in lovingkindness.
May all beings accept themselves just as they are.
May all beings be free from danger, worry, tension, anger, and fear.
May all beings have courage and confidence.
May all beings be happy and healthy.
May all beings touch great and natural peace.
May all beings know the joy of being alive.
May all beings' lives be of benefit to all other beings.
May all beings' hearts and minds awaken; may all beings be free.

Short Version

May I be filled with lovingkindness; may I be held in lovingkindness.
May I be free from danger.
May I be happy and healthy.
May I be at peace.

May you be filled with lovingkindness; may you be held in lovingkindness.
May you be free from danger.
May you be happy and healthy.
May you be at peace.

May all beings be filled with lovingkindness; may all beings be held in lovingkindness.

May all beings be free from danger.
May all beings be happy and healthy.
May all beings be at peace.

Bibliography

THE following books are ones that have touched my life and held meaning for me. As space is limited, these are only a few of the many authors who have spoken to my heart. In addition, some of the authors mentioned here have written other valuable books not listed. Hopefully this initial list will be helpful to you on your journey.

Abibio-Clottey, Aeesha, and Kokomon Clottey. *Beyond Fear: Twelve Spiritual Keys to Racial Healing.* Tiburon, CA: H. J. Kramer, 1998.

Bloch, Douglas. *I am with You Always: A Treasury of Inspirational Quotations, Poems, and Prayers.* New York: Bantam, 1992.

Brach, Tara., *Radical Acceptance: Embracing Your Life with the Heart of a Buddha.* New York: Bantam, 2003.

Chodron, Pema. *The Places that Scare You: A Guide to Fearlessness in Difficult Times.* Boston: Shambhala, 2001.

Duff, Kat. *The Alchemy of Illness.* New York: Pantheon, 1993.

Dyer, Wayne. *Change Your Thoughts, Change Your Life: Living the Wisdom of the Tao.* Carlsbad, CA: Hay House, 2007.

——. *Real Magic: Creating Miracles in Everyday Life.* New York: HarperCollins, 1991.

Eadie, Betty. *Embraced by the Light.* Placerville, CA: Gold Leaf Press, 1992.

Ford, Debbie. *The Dark Side of the Light Chasers.* New York: Riverhead, 1998.

Foundation for Inner Peace. *A Course in Miracles.* Mill Valley, CA: Foundation for Inner Peace, 1975, 1985.

Gray, John. *Men Are from Mars, Women Are from Venus: A Practical Guide for Improving Communication and Getting What You Want in Your Relationships.* New York: HarperCollins, 1992.

Hanh, Thich Nhat. Being Peace. Berkeley, CA: Parallax Press, 1987.

Hawkins, David. *Power vs. Force: The Hidden Determinants of Human Behavior.* Carlsbad, CA: Hay House, 2002.

Hay, Louise. *The Power Is Within You.* Carson, CA: Hay House, 1991.

Hendrix, Harville. *Getting the Love You Want: A Guide for Couples.* New York: H. Holt, 1988.

Hicks, Esther, and Jerry Hicks. *Ask and It Is Given: Learning to Manifest Your Desires.* Carlsbad, CA: Hay House, 2004.

Jampolsky, Gerald. *Love Is Letting Go of Fear.* Millbrae, CA: Celestial Arts, 1979.

——. *Teach Only Love: The Twelve Principles of Attitudinal Healing.* Hillsboro, OR: Beyond Words, 2000.

Jampolsky, Gerald, and Diane Cirincione. *Change Your Mind, Change Your Life: Concepts in Attitudinal Healing.* New York: Bantam Books, 1993.

Kabat-Zinn, Jon. *Full Catastrophe Living: Using the Wisdom of Your Body and Mind to Face Stress, Pain, and Illness.* New York: Delacorte, 1990.

Levine, Stephen. *A Gradual Awakening.* Garden City, NY: Anchor Press, 1979, 1989.

Osteen, Joel. *Become a Better You: 7 Keys to Improving Your Life Every Day.* New York: Free Press, 2007.

Page, Susan. *How One of You Can Bring the Two of You Together:*

Breakthrough Strategies to Resolve Your Conflicts and Reignite Your Love. New York: Broadway Books, 1997.

Patent, Arnold. *You Can Have It All: The Art of Winning the Money Game and Living a Life of Joy.* Great Neck, NY: Money Mastery, 1984, 1987.

Peirce, Penney. *The Intuitive Way: A Guide to Living from Inner Wisdom. Hillsboro, OR: Beyond Words,* 1997.

Roman, Sonaya. *Living with Joy.* H.J. Kramer, Inc., Tiburon, CA, 1986.

Rosenberg, Marshall B. *Nonviolent Communication: A Language of Compassion.* Del Mar, CA: PuddleDancer Press, 1999.

Tolle, Eckhart. *The Power of Now: A Guide to Spiritual Enlightenment.* Novato, CA: New World Library, 1999.

Topf, Linda Noble. *You Are Not Your Illness: Seven Principles for Meeting the Challenge.* New York: Simon & Schuster, 1995.

Williamson, Marianne. *A Return to Love: Reflections on the Principles of A Course in Miracles.* New York: HarperCollins, 1992.

——. *Illuminata: Thoughts, Prayers, Rites of Passage.* New York: Random House, 1994.

Yogananda, Paramahansa, *Where There Is Light: Insight and Inspiration for Meeting Life's Challenges.* Los Angeles, CA: Self-Realization Fellowship, 1988, 1994.

About the Author
Laurie Pappas, PhD

DR. Laurie Pappas, an educator, counselor, trained mediator, speaker, writer, and metaphysician, was the co-founder of the Metro Detroit Center for Attitudinal Healing, and directed the activities of the center for sixteen years. She has also conducted spiritual/metaphysical, counseling sessions for twenty years. Dr. Pappas has taught classes and workshops and trained personal growth group leaders during this period of time, in addition to having been a frequent columnist in a large Detroit metaphysical newspaper in the early 1990s.

As a young adult, while Laurie worked in elementary education, she began her search for the underlying causes of disharmony and discord among school children. Several years later, community service work for the hungry and homeless brought her attention to the role that the mind plays in creating abundance or scarcity, peace or conflict. These experiences led her first to the field of guidance and counseling and eventually to the study of metaphysics, where she was able to obtain satisfying answers to her questions and workable solutions to many of life's challenges.

In the spring of 2005, Laurie was program chairperson of the 7th Annual Conference on Nonviolence, Peace, and Prosperity held in Detroit. She is a recipient of the 2005 International Peace Prize, Key of Success Award, and Woman of the Year Award, bestowed by the United Cultural Convention of the United States of America for outstanding personal achievements to the good of society as a whole. Dr. Pappas is committed to the inspiration and growth of all those with whom she has the honor of working and to the creation of cultures grounded in harmony, peace, compassion, and love.

Breinigsville, PA USA
09 December 2010
251044BV00005B/43/P